CREATE YOUR ALIGNED BUSINESS

Your
Step-by-Step
Guide
to Purpose
and Profit
Through
Human Design

ANNA NICHOLS, MBA

Edited by Anna Paradox and Laurie Knight
Cover Design by Kristina Edstrom

Human Design Press, an Imprint for GracePoint Publishing (www.GracePointPublishing.com)

HUMAN DESIGN PRESS

GracePoint Matrix, LLC
624 S. Cascade Ave, Suite 201, Colorado Springs, CO 80903
www.GracePointMatrix.com Email: Admin@GracePointMatrix.com
SAN # 991-6032

A Library of Congress Control Number has been requested and is pending.

ISBN: 978-1-966346-05-0
eISBN: 978-1-966346-66-1

Books may be purchased for educational, business, or sales promotional use.
For distribution queries contact Sales@IPGbook.com
For non-retail bulk order requests contact Orders@GracePointPublishing.com

Printed in U.S.A

TABLE OF CONTENTS

To my family and friends:

Your love, encouragement, and belief in me made this journey possible. Thank you for walking beside me through every chapter of my life and business.

And to the visionaries holding this book in your hands:

This book was written for you because *business is not a guessing game. It's all about alignment.* May these words ignite the clarity, direction, and confidence you need to bring your boldest business visions to life and create the legacy only you were born to build.

PREFACE

In my first summer as an entrepreneur, I remember sitting in my home office (which was a small desk in the corner of my kids' playroom), trying to decide in what direction to go next in business. The room smelled of rotten milk, spilled countless times on the floor by my kids, mixed with the lilac scented candle I was using to cover it up. At that time, I had been building my coaching business for almost a year. I had joined several online coaching programs and felt like I had gotten in over my head, with each one pointing me in a different direction, promising their way was the "best" way to build an online business. Yet in each one, I felt resistance to the business models and strategies they were teaching. That afternoon, after a long cry and wondering if I was even meant for entrepreneurship, I was flipping through one of the many Human Design books I had purchased, trying to understand myself at a deeper level and searching for answers that felt aligned to me.

Suddenly, I sat up straighter in my chair as I started reading about my Human Design Environment. *OMG! This* was the reason I felt so out of alignment with the way I was building my business. I could clearly see that my business model, services, marketing, and sales process were completely out of alignment with my Human Design Environment and suddenly I didn't feel like a failure in business. I realized the model I was trying to build was not aligned to me. Prior to that moment, I had thought Human Design was meant for personal development, but my business brain *knew* there had to be more. With a master's degree in business, having parents who had owned several businesses themselves, helping small local businesses and large corporate organizations, I knew planning was a foundational part of starting a successful business. So, I jumped online and began searching for "business planning through Human Design." The results came up with fun concepts, but no step-by-step process on how to properly plan a purposeful and profitable business. This began my journey which ultimately led to my writing this book.

I spent the following year obsessively studying Human Design and searching for information on how to build a business the way I learned in college and in my experience doing this work with local businesses. There are thousands of books on traditional business planning and hundreds of business development centers in communities across America, and all of them have the same fundamental pieces included. The components of a business plan are the fundamental building blocks of successful businesses, yet traditional business planning was missing one huge thing: *soul alignment*. I saw so many entrepreneurs trying to build businesses that didn't feel right or guessing at who they wanted to serve or how to serve them. They knew they wanted to be entrepreneurs but were unsure about the right path for them.

This was when I realized that the connection had never been made in this way. No one had bridged traditional step-by-step business planning with Human Design. And the calling on my heart, the one my soul kept showing me, was to help entrepreneurs practically plan out their businesses so they could begin building them and stop wasting time and energy doing things that are not aligned with that vision. I wanted both the practical business strategy *and* the soul-aligned mission. So did all of my clients and all the spiritually awakened entrepreneurs I talked with. I wanted purposeful and I wanted profitable. And if you are reading this book, my guess is you do too. After scouring the internet for books on comprehensive business planning based on Human Design, I knew I had to write it. Through experiencing tremendous frustration, continuing to wish for something that did not exist at the time, continuing to deepen my Human Design understanding, and making connections to business in a way I didn't see others sharing, I finally realized I was meant to bring this vision to life.

The book you are about to read, *Creating Your Aligned Business*, was purposefully inspired and structured by the components of traditional business planning infused with the wisdom of Human Design through an entrepreneur lens. The information synthesizes what I have learned through my formal education with my experience participating in numerous coaching programs and mixed with insights gleaned from various Human Design teachers. Based on this, I provide personal interpretations of each business element and Human Design element, in an attempt to bridge traditional business concepts with the wisdom of Human Design. This is not a basic book on Human Design fundamentals. If you are new to Human Design and already interested in this book, I recommend getting a foundational Human Design guide in addition to this book. You can access a free basic Human Design chart at spiritualbusinessincubator.com/hdchart and for an in-depth report that thoroughly covers and supports the discussion in this book, order your personalized Entrepreneur by Design report, which is my advanced analysis of Human Design through the lens of entrepreneurship at spiritualbusinessincubator.com/business-report. I share my favorite foundational books and Human Design teachings in the Resources Section at the end of this book.

It's also important to state that this book is organized by the components of a business plan, not by the aspects of Human Design because the order in which you create your plan matters. You cannot start at the end and hop around—well you can, but you may likely feel confused about what you are creating and how you are going to create it. This is intentional because the purpose is to help you understand business planning concepts better and also understand which part of Human Design I use when helping people organize the different parts of their businesses. It is intentional because just like building a house, you would not start with the roof before laying the foundation. This means you will see me refer to the aspects of Human Design (e.g. Type, Profile, Environment, centers, etc.) multiple times throughout the book. In some cases, I give explanations on how those aspects may influence your business protocols (like using specific gates to help you guide offers), and in other cases, I share which parts of Human Design I use in that process. If I were to include everything in one book, it would be thousands of pages. The point of this book is to give you a strong, aligned foundation for the future of your business. If you are searching for more information in any of the areas, you can access additional business planning resources and programs at spiritualbusinessincubator.com/services.

Ultimately, there are many ways to design a business. This book will help you explore all of the critical components of business through both a practical lens and a Human Design lens. It will introduce how different parts of your Human Design could shape or help you define these components with more ease in the business planning process. My hope for you is that you get clarity on exactly the right business you are meant to build and know that all pieces of your business plan are aligned to you!

CHAPTER 1

THE BIG PICTURE: INTRODUCTION TO HUMAN DESIGN IN BUSINESS

The Big Picture

One of the most important questions every entrepreneur needs to answer at the very beginning is "why am I starting a business?" Some of you may have always dreamed of being a business owner, while others pursued entrepreneurship as a pivot away from a corporate job. Deep in my soul, I have known my whole life that I would have my own business. However, figuring out the right business for me was a messy experience that ultimately became clear through understanding my unique Human Design. As an ambitious, smart, and hardworking woman, I knew that I could achieve anything I set my mind to; however, when I started understanding and listening to my Sacral Authority, I learned that just because I *can* do something does not mean it is in alignment. Getting clarity on the right business to build, one that would fulfill the mission of my heart while also being profitable and sustainable in the long run, came from the beautiful blending of Human Design with strategic business planning.

I was raised by Polish immigrants who believed that if you worked hard, you would create a better life. This became one of my deeply rooted subconscious beliefs. Don't get me wrong, I love the feeling of accomplishing something through grit and hard work, but somewhere along the way I realized that working hard was not the same as working intentionally and in alignment. This realization was the catalyst for a ton of changes that profoundly shifted the direction of my life.

I share this book with you because I want you to go into entrepreneurship with your eyes wide open. The entrepreneurial journey is not for the faint of heart. To be successful, you must grow and push yourself to expand in ways you are both terrified of and that are necessary. Your identity will evolve many times. Your knowledge, skills, and abilities will also have to evolve. This book is the entrepreneur user manual I wish had existed when I started my career. It's the process I still refer to when consciously planning out the next evolution of my business. The process of strategic business planning is critical for success, and my hope is to make it simple, fun, and effective in order to help you make a greater impact in less time!

Fun fact about me: I love spreadsheets! Understanding numbers and seeing patterns is my jam, but I know this is not most people's cup of tea. I want to share with you some statistics that may help you understand the importance of creating a clear, written business plan. According to the US Department of Trade, businesses are 260 percent more likely to launch with a written business plan. And still only 33 percent of solopreneurs and small businesses actually have created such a document. Why is that? I contemplated this question for a long time. Eventually, I realized that although business and strategic planning were my gifts, most entrepreneurs are more passionate about the unique way they serve people, and the business stuff felt scary, overwhelming, and unimportant in the beginning.

In my experience, many entrepreneurs see slow income and impact growth due to not having a clear vision of the specific type of business they are actually creating. I remember feeling this deeply when I first started my entrepreneurial journey. I felt so passionate about helping people and thought I had the perfect plan to make that happen. The reality was quite different, but that core intention has fueled my actions ever since. I also thrive on the great feeling of relief of knowing exactly what I am creating and how I am going to do it. Mapping out that clear vision gave me the same endorphin release as when I reach the top of a mountain after hiking for hours.

I have worked with entrepreneurs and small businesses in many industries, including local brick and mortar as well as fully online businesses. My experience includes supporting healers, acupuncturists, life coaches, community builders, hospitality agencies, dog trainers, mortgage lenders, and bookkeepers to name a few. I have observed a common theme among them—few of them started with an intentional business plan and all had to hustle their way to success. Working hard was seen as honorable in the world I grew up in. My parents (both Projectors) owned multiple local motels and were the most exhausted humans I have ever met. I know my family is only one of many similar stories. My parents' friends all also owned businesses—including hospitality, restaurants, construction, and housecleaning. My husband's family are multi-generational pioneer ranchers and farmers in Colorado, working hard on the land and making (almost) everything from scratch. Hard work has always been a symbol of success and pride all around me. Does this sound familiar?

Growing up, my family poured their hearts into owning a local motel, working tirelessly to make it succeed. They owned this business from when I was eight years old until when they sold it a few months before my twentieth birthday. During those years, I remember that every Thanksgiving and Christmas, my parents would take me and my younger sister and brother to work with them, so their employees could take the holidays off. My siblings and I worked in my parents' business when we were not in school, and having this experience fundamentally shaped my life. This was my first exposure to entrepreneurship, and that level of service deeply imprinted in my subconscious. This was the first, but not the last, experience in my life where it was reinforced that hard work equals service and as a Generator, I am good at working hard.

So, I went to college thinking this would help me find my path, and I studied finance and ultimately received a master's degree in business. During this time, I had amazing opportunities to lead large-scale organizational development projects in the areas of accounting, financial aid, academic advising, and registration. I obsessively studied leadership and coached aspiring leaders, all wanting to do good in the world. I landed highly sought-after jobs in leadership and management positions at local and national organizations, climbing the corporate ladder and hoping to make a bigger impact in the organizations which I served. I had done all the "right" things, at least in the areas I was conditioned to think would lead to success. Yet despite achieving a six-figure salary and promotions every eighteen months, I was still working hard, felt stifled by limited opportunities, lacked support, and believed I had no control over my actions and decisions.

All the while, my parents would often send me to their Polish friends to implement systems n their businesses that would ultimately help them make more money. Helping businesses of any kind grow has been a common theme throughout my whole life.

Now, I can see in my Human Design and Gene Keys that I was born to be an entrepreneur. This explains the deep inner knowing that I have had my whole life that I am an entrepreneur. Eventually there came a point in 2021 when I couldn't ignore the calling anymore and I took the leap to leave my honorable career to become an entrepreneur.

Upon making this leap, I was quickly slapped in the face with the realization that my entire identity had been defined by my career. This was compounded by the fact that I was extremely burnt out and had been living with untreated PTSD and postpartum depression, which made my flight response extremely high every time I tried to take steps forward in my business. Regardless, I pushed forward, slowly but surely, because I was determined to help people and succeed as an entrepreneur.

I thought I had a solid business plan when I began helping local entrepreneurs grow their businesses and prepare to either sell or pass them down to maximize their return on investment (ROI) in a lifetime of hard work. I had started to sign local businesses as clients, and despite knowing exactly how I thought I "should" be showing up to grow my business, something still felt off.

I remember the repetitive thoughts of *I am not aligned*, which ultimately led me to finding and joining my first online personal development program. This is where I discovered Human Design. *Hallelujah!* Although this book is not about healing, per se, finding Human Design was the catalyst that urged me to see a glimmer of who I knew myself to be on the inside and to start unraveling the deep layers of conditioning that made me think there was a "right" way to do everything. This also started my healing journey, which has led me to regulating my nervous system, reprogramming my subconscious, raising my vibration, and initiating a series of spiritual awakenings that opened my channels and unlocked my spiritual gifts.

My time became consumed with growing a business while obsessively studying Human Design, initially to get clarity on myself. I am a 5/2 Sacral Generator and when I first learned about Human Design, I felt seen, but at the same time, I realized I was only a fraction of who I am truly *designed* to be. I knew I was meant to help people in a big way, but was not sure how I would do it. So, I kept learning about myself and trusted I would figure it out.

What Kind of Business Are You Building?

I believe you're here because you feel called to create a business that is about more than just making money—it's purposeful, sustainable, and aligned with the calling on your heart to make the world a better place in your unique way, from who you truly are. Of course profitability is a fundamental reason I believe business planning is important, but aligned business planning is what makes a business both purposeful and profitable. As you go through this book, I hope you'll look at the big picture of your business to find the clarity and direction that so many of us search for when starting the entrepreneurial journey. Many invest a significant amount of time, energy, and money before they have the clarity they desire. Because when you have a calling to help others, it's easy to get lost in the process of how to do that in a sustainable and profitable way.

My first online program exposed me to the possibilities of online entrepreneurship, which I appreciated since I had spent most of my life in a small city in western Colorado. I already understood the concept of strategic business planning but had previously approached that process through the lens of local business, large organizations, and nonprofits. When I decided to shift my fully in-person coaching venture into the online space, I thought I would sign up with a business coach who would take me through a process to grow my online business. I remember them advertising something like "The Complete Playbook on How to Create an Online Business," so I was hooked and signed up. Growing an online business seemed so intimidating and also so exciting, and I jumped in with both feet to learn so I could get to helping even more people than I would meet in my small town.

A short while into the program, I felt a tremendous amount of frustration and resistance in developing this signature program model that the coach was promoting as "the best way" to build an online business. Her model left me confused about who I was supposed to help and how I would help them in the online space, which I was told had to be some ultra-specific niche with an ultra-specific problem that I would solve. This wasn't how I had grown my local business, but I understood that growing a business online was different, so I kept trying to force myself to do what I was being instructed to do. I felt like a total failure. Then one day while excessively scrolling Instagram, I found another business coach promoting that *their* process was so successful that they promised I would make my "first online sale in fourteen days." They also promised a 100 percent money-back guarantee if I didn't make back my $10,000 investment during the six-month program. Not only did neither of those things happen, but because I didn't read the fine print of their very one-sided contract, I was stuck in a program that was not right for me. I was frustrated, mad at myself, and honestly embarrassed for being so naïve. Their model was promoted as "the best at getting clients online" but actually left my bank account drained and my self-doubt at an all-time high. I still hadn't established any online clients, and I continued to find clients locally and successfully supported them the way I had done before ever embarking on building an online business. I wasn't ready to give up online, but something wasn't working and I was determined to figure it out. What I eventually realized is that I was piecemealing my online business together and not building it using the foundations I knew were the key to building a successful business locally. In case you are wondering, business fundamentals are critically important no matter what kind of business you are building… and these are what you are going to learn about in this book.

I share this with you not to bash anyone, because I want to believe their intentions were good. They too were wanting to share their gifts and help people. However, what they were teaching was what worked for them and not what was right for me and my mission. Finally came a moment for me (and maybe now you) that I knew the season of hopping from coach to coach, or from this offer to that offer, or starting a bunch of things that didn't feel right was over. It was sometime while I was in the middle of these two programs, hoping I could string something together, that I was also reading a Human Design book talking about Environments. I was reading this because I wanted to make my home more aligned to my Markets Environment when I had the biggest *aha* of my entrepreneurial journey. This moment gave me the clarity of why neither of these prior programs worked for me and why I felt so much resistance. It was because I was not building the right business according to *my* Human Design.

The more I learned about Human Design, the more I understood my uniqueness as a person. With all of my formal business education and experience, I started to interpret the components of Human Design through the lens of business. I did this at an intellectual level for a long time before I began embodying it, because, well, I still had a lot of conditioning clouding my being and deep limiting beliefs about who I was and what I was meant to do in this world.

I thought back to my original business plan and all the ones I had helped people create throughout my life. They had the components that could create a profitable business, but they were missing one huge thing: alignment to Human Design. This is why something kept feeling off and why that inner calling kept screaming to be heard. The more I studied Human Design, the more I knew I was *designed* in this way for a specific purpose. This system was so much more than an explanation of who I was, and it had insights into my sacred mission and how I was meant to achieve that with the most flow. As an entrepreneur at heart, I knew I would be fulfilling my sacred mission through building a business and through helping others build theirs. I finally had the clarity for exactly how I was going to do that.

What I craved was a path truly aligned to me. I wanted a roadmap that was tailored to me and not one-size-fits-all. I wanted that for me, and I want that now for you. My path ultimately led me to realizing I am here to add to the body of knowledge that is Human Design, a system that allowed me to understand myself and my purpose in a way that nothing else had. But while existing Human Design information provided insight, what I couldn't find was a guide that combined this spiritual wisdom with the practical, step-by-step planning I knew from the business world. That's what this book is.

Developing a Clear Vision for Your Business

It is essential that you have a clear picture of what kind of business you want to build. Although many entrepreneurs start out as solopreneurs wanting to share their gifts, they first focus in on serving people, versus really consciously thinking about the mission of the business as an entity and which business model would best support meeting that mission. It's easy to get overwhelmed with the sheer number of options and strategies available. How do you even know which one is right for you? This book is 100 percent going to help you see a plethora of options for you to consciously consider when choosing how to fulfill your mission. The modern entrepreneurial landscape is brimming with enticing courses, mentorships, business models, and marketing trends, but navigating this sea of choices without a grounded vision can lead to frustration and burnout, and a lot of wasted time, energy, and money.

One of the most common pitfalls that entrepreneurs face is investing in coaches, programs, or team members that are not aligned with them or the mission of their business. This could lead to a significant amount of wasted resources building a business that is not right for your Human Design and not the best business structure for your specific vision and mission. This often happens because mission-driven, heart-centered entrepreneurs are focused on their mission and may become swayed by marketing hype, bold promises of short cuts to success, or genuine desire to serve clients and make a difference. Your mission is important to your soul, and if you are reading this book, I believe you are deeply called to make a positive impact in the world. While well-intentioned, there comes a moment when you realize that you need more support and structure to make sure you are taken care of for the long term.

A great example of this is when I worked with a woman whose heart was called to creating a diverse, inclusive, and accessible community space for spiritual guides, healers, and practitioners. At its core, her business model was based on renting out the most beautiful and energetically clean commercial rental space to people to run workshops, healing experiences, and deep transformational work for individual and group sessions. Because she was so committed to this being more than simply rental space, she was offering many things to the practitioners in her community for free or very low cost. She came to me with her business making very little profit and she was not paying herself at all. She was doing whatever she could in order to keep the business afloat because her primary focus was always on serving her community. Her realization was that she hadn't built something that was sustainable for the long term from a business perspective. Once we started going through my signature business planning process together, I was able to show her that the mission on her heart was not just a wild idea, but rather actually part of her Human Design. This helped her connect with her mission even deeper and see the grand, expansive vision she was minimizing because her current finances were not where she wanted them to be. Once she got a clear vision of what she actually wanted to build, we explored different business models that would support her mission and bring money into the business while maintaining the free and affordable services she wanted to provide her clients. In the end, she decided to switch her business from a for-profit model to a nonprofit model. This changed how she approached the idea of bringing in money to her business, and we wrote an aligned business plan that supported her in pursuing grants and donations to fund her business mission.

Previously, this woman had joined other business coaching programs where she was encouraged to raise her prices or create offerings that did not feel in alignment for her or her heart's mission. And because they were not in alignment, she was not implementing any of them, and therefore, she continued to feel frustrated about her business. By finally getting true clarity on her vision, we were able to create an aligned business plan that moved her business forward in a way that was profitable and sustainable.

The Challenge of Decision-Making in Entrepreneurship

Two of the hardest parts of entrepreneurship are making decisions and taking consistent action. At the same time, these are also the most important parts of entrepreneurship because without decisions and action, there is no progress. The decision-making process is influenced by multiple factors (including emotions, resource availability, and desired timeline, among others). Understanding your unique way of doing this can empower more strategic and aligned decision-making.

- **Lack of Alignment:** Many entrepreneurs, especially in the early stage of business, adopt a scattered approach, offering their services to anyone and everyone in an attempt to generate income. While understandable, this approach can lead to constantly chasing the dollar, which is a surefire path to burnout and disconnect from your true mission. By shifting your focus to intentional, mission-driven action, you can sustain your energy and passion. This alignment fuels creativity and abundance, enabling you to create with greater flow and enthusiasm, no matter your Human Design Type.

- **Societal and Generational Conditioning:** Beyond the strategic choices you make, there's the added layer of societal and generational conditioning that can impact your mindset. From a young age, people are influenced by narratives about success, work ethic, and worthiness. These inherited beliefs often create limiting perceptions and self-doubt that are just as heavy to overcome as any strategic misstep.

My hope for you is to achieve such clarity about your business vision that, once your written business plan is complete, you will have unwavering confidence in every decision you make and every action you take moving forward. This clarity will become your anchor, allowing you to filter out distractions and stay committed to your true path.

Human Design Through a Business Lens

Human Design is a profound self-discovery system that combines elements of both ancient and modern wisdom. It integrates astrology, Hindu chakra system, I Ching, Kabbalah, and quantum physics. I believe your Human Design can be viewed as your cosmic job description. It reveals your unique life mission and the specific gifts, strengths, and traits you possess to fulfill it. This is not just a roadmap for self-discovery; it's an empowering framework for aligning your business decisions with your true nature.

Many aspects of your unique Human Design can give you insights into how you are meant to be most aligned as an entrepreneur as well as what you are meant to do to fulfill your sacred mission in this lifetime. I utilize many aspects of Human Design in my programs and in working with clients to design their aligned businesses. We will cover how many of these are used throughout the book, but here is a quick overview:

- **Energy Type:** How you energetically interact with other people.
- **Signature Theme:** How you know if something is aligned.
- **Not-Self Theme:** How you know if something is not aligned.
- **Authority:** How you make decisions.

- **Strategy:** How you take action.
- **Profile:** The role that you are designed to play.
- **Centers:** Themes of consistent energy you have.
- **Gates:** The gifts you are here to give or receive.
- **Channels:** Strong combinations of gifts that provide direction.
- **Environment:** Represents the vibe you feel most comfortable with and confident in.
- **Incarnation Cross:** Your life purpose, also known as sacred mission.

Although these are not all of the components of Human Design, I focus on these when designing a business. In this book, I share insights on how specific aspects directly apply to entrepreneurship, but I do not provide a comprehensive explanation for every aspect of each person's Human Design. I have created a comprehensive report where you can get your personalized information about your specific chart details here: spiritualbusinessincubator.com/business-report

Your Soul's Mission

You are not here by accident. According to Human Design, your soul mission is one that you've chosen, and you have been equipped with the exact tools and qualities needed to carry it out. The elements of your design, whether defined or undefined centers, channels, or gates and more, act as the perfect tool belt for navigating your entrepreneurial journey.

This design is intentional, allowing you to achieve your mission with the most joy, flow, and freedom possible. Recognizing this unique blueprint helps you build a business that aligns with your true essence, freeing you from the pressures of comparison and conventional expectations. By applying your Human Design to your business, you create a sustainable path that is not only profitable but also deeply fulfilling.

There's a proven way to turn more of your Human Design into a viable business: creating an aligned business plan, or "Aligned Business

Blueprint™" as I call it. Research in *Small Business Economics* revealed that entrepreneurs who take the time to plan are 152 percent more likely to launch their businesses and 129 percent more likely to keep growing beyond the initial startup phase. Why? Because a written business plan provides focus, accountability, and resilience through challenges. When you have a plan that is aligned with your unique Human Design, you know you will get to your goal, and you are no longer distracted by shiny objects. By intentionally mapping out each component of your plan, you will know exactly where to invest your time, energy, and money and know that it's getting you closer to making your business vision a reality.

Every strategy out there works, but which ones are right for you? The key is finding the ones that work specifically for your Human Design. This is not about doing more; it's about getting clear so you can intentionally focus on aligned things with confidence.

As you design your business, I encourage you to ask, "What is the highest service I can offer the world?" I believe the more good-hearted people succeed, the more positive change we can bring about. Imagine the impact of more money and success in the hands of people like you who are dedicated to making a difference. This is the foundation for everything in these pages.

This book is for you if you're an entrepreneur who loves Human Design and wants your business to reflect that alignment. You're likely someone who values working smarter, not harder, and desires a step-by-step process grounded in both practical strategy and spiritual alignment.

You're not interested in just any business tactics; you want something proven, but it's important to be infused with purpose. You may feel a deep mission to make the world a better place, to raise the vibration of the collective. You want to work from a place of service, sharing your gifts, skills, and wisdom. Yet, you might feel unclear on how to organize these talents or even how to turn your vision into reality.

If you've been brainstorming ideas, following every new trend, you might feel as if nothing has fully clicked. Perhaps you're uncertain if the work you're doing is truly your path. Or perhaps you want a sustainable, profitable business that supports the life you desire, but you are not sure how to be intentional and make it long-lasting, not just another attempt at success.

In the chapters ahead, you'll find practical, actionable ways to bring your Human Design into your business, creating something that not only serves your clients but also deeply fulfills you.

Return to this book (and your business plan) anytime you need a check-in to see if you're on track. These steps aren't just a beginning; they're tools to realign and redirect whenever you need. Here, you'll learn to approach business with intentionality—working smarter, not harder—by focusing only on what's aligned with your Human Design and your unique goals.

Key Components of Your Aligned Business Blueprint

Throughout this book, we will explore the main components of the business planning process through the lens of practical business strategies as well as specific Human Design elements. As the leader of your business, you need to design and make informed decisions on each of these. Each section builds upon the previous one, and I have created a cohesive framework called the "Aligned Business Blueprint." This includes the following components which we will discuss in order throughout this book:

- **Mission Statement:** The reason your business exists. The core mission that sets the foundation for everything you do in your business.
- **Value Proposition:** Definition of the unique value you bring to the market.
- **Business Assessment:** Take an honest look at your current business landscape, strengths, and areas for growth to understand where you are starting from.

- **Future Business Vision:** Envision the long-term goals and the direction of your business to provide a clear target to work toward.
- **Niche:** Identify your specific target audience and the unique problems you solve to position yourself effectively in the market.
- **Business Model:** Determine the structure and approach your business will take to generate revenue and deliver value.
- **Services and Offers:** Design your products or services to align with your mission and meet the needs of your niche.
- **Messaging:** Craft a clear and compelling message that communicates your value proposition and resonates with your audience.
- **Marketing:** Develop strategies for promoting your business and reaching your target audience in a way that aligns with your values.
- **Sales:** Create a sales process that feels authentic and is effective in converting potential clients into loyal customers.
- **Organizational Structure:** Outline how your team and roles are structured to support your business operations and growth.
- **Resources and Financial Plan:** Plan your budget, resources, and financial strategy to ensure sustainability and growth.

These elements are interdependent; if you skip steps or jump around without going through them in sequence, you may still find yourself out of alignment. Each component influences the next, creating a comprehensive and unified approach to your business strategy.

Creating a business without a plan is a bit like trying to build a house without a blueprint. Imagine for a moment you're building your dream home. You wouldn't just start pouring concrete or putting up walls without a clear vision of the house you want, would you? Instead, you'd start with a solid plan, a blueprint that outlines every detail, from the number of rooms and windows to the overall vibe of the place. Maybe you're going for something luxurious, something cozy, or maybe something cost-effective. Whatever your vision, a clear plan will bring it to life in a way that's strong, stable, and aligned with what you truly want.

Without a business plan, you might have a beautiful vision of helping people or creating change, but you'd lack the details to bring that vision to life in a way that's efficient and sustainable. Your plan is the map that keeps you aligned, using your resources wisely so you're not just building something beautiful but also something that can stand the test of time and support you fully.

In business, especially as an online entrepreneur, it's the same. An aligned plan acts as the architectural blueprint that truly serves both your purpose and your goals. Think of it as creating an environment that's not just profitable but also sustainable and fulfilling. The time you spend mapping out your business model, services, and mission is time spent creating a foundation that will keep you grounded, no matter how complex or busy things get. By envisioning every component, from the way you will attract clients to the full customer journey— and especially the financial projections—you set yourself up to grow with purpose and direction, avoiding the trap of hustling endlessly without desired results.

Without a clear plan, you may have an idea of what you want to achieve or how you want to impact others, but you'll lack the steps, structure, and strategy to bring it to life in the most aligned way possible. It becomes easier to fall into the cycle of endless trial and error, draining your time, energy, and finances without creating the business you truly want. Here are two specific examples in the world of online entrepreneurship that highlight why having an aligned business plan is crucial.

Example One: Launching an Online Coaching Program

Let's say you're an online coach with a deep desire to help clients achieve personal transformation. Without a well-thought-out plan, you might create a program based on what you *think* people want. Without doing market research, deciding on strategic pricing, or implementing a step-by-step launch strategy, you risk investing countless hours developing something that doesn't quite resonate with your audience. Now, imagine instead that you've created a business plan that aligns with your Human Design and core mission. Your plan guides you to choose a niche you're energetically aligned with, to price your program at a rate that feels good to say out loud and actually delivers result to your clients, and to create a launch sequence that plays to your strengths. By having these foundational elements mapped out, you're not just selling a program, you're creating a business pillar designed with sustainability and ease in mind, reducing burnout and enhancing client impact.

Example Two: Building a Digital Product Library

Picture yourself as a content creator who dreams of building a library of digital products that serve a diverse community of clients. Without a structured plan, you might end up creating products sporadically based on inspiration or trends, each lacking a cohesive brand voice or value ladder. This can lead to incohesive offerings that confuse potential customers, making it hard for them to understand your brand or recognize your expertise. With an aligned business plan, you'd approach the digital product library with a clear structure. Perhaps your Human Design says you thrive on creating detailed resources, so your plan would outline a product creation timeline that aligns with your energy cycles. You'd define your ideal customer, the specific problem each product will solve, and the way each product guides clients to the next level of their journey with you. This intentional approach creates a magnetic brand presence with products that naturally flow from one to the next, helping you build authority while also feeling empowered by the work you're doing.

In both examples, an aligned business plan allows you to make clear, confident decisions up front, preventing wasted resources and ensuring that your business reflects your unique vision and purpose. When you design with intention, you set the stage for a business that grows in harmony with your energy and values. By creating a strong foundation through careful planning, you gain a sense of direction and clarity that transforms your business from a random assortment of ideas into a cohesive, powerful force that supports you as much as it serves your clients.

Your business plan is the blueprint that anchors your vision, allowing you to focus on what truly matters while cutting through the noise of endless options. By thoughtfully mapping out your Aligned Business Blueprint, you create a business that not only fulfills your purpose but also brings ease and joy into your life, aligning with your unique path and paving the way for long-term success. Now let's dive in!

Chapter 2

YOUR BUSINESS MISSION AND UNIQUE VALUE PROPOSITION

What Is a Mission Statement?

A mission statement is the foundation of your business; it defines why your "it" exists, who you serve, and how you create impact. It's more than just a sentence; it's the guiding force behind every decision, strategy, and action you take. Without a clear mission, businesses can easily lose focus, chasing trends or opportunities that don't align with their deeper purpose. Defining your mission first ensures that everything you build (your offers, marketing, messaging, and partnerships) stems from a place of alignment and clarity. It acts as your North Star, helping you stay on track and ensuring you create a business that feels purposeful, fulfilling, and sustainable. Before you think about branding, services, or scaling, take the time to define your mission, because everything else will flow more effortlessly when you get crystal clear on your why.

What Is Your Unique Value Proposition?

Your unique value proposition is the sparkle in your business. It defines what makes you unique in the marketplace, why you stand out, and how you serve your clients in a way only you can. When you have a calling on your heart, a sense that you are meant to create something but aren't sure what it is, your value proposition becomes the process to clarify your cosmic mission, life purpose, and the unique gifts you bring to the world.

Imagine this as the foundation of a house. Without a clear value proposition, your business may feel like it's built on unstable ground, vulnerable to the winds of distraction, overwhelm, and misalignment. With a strong mission statement and value proposition, you have a solid base from which you can grow confidently, knowing every decision you make and action you take are aligned with your purpose and strengths. Defining these helps you with the following:

- **No More Guessing:** Clear value proposition provides the framework for understanding what you are here to create and how your unique energy aligns with this creation. When you understand this, you're no longer guessing; you're building with intention.

- **Stand Out in the Market:** Knowing what makes you and your business unique allows you to communicate effectively with potential clients and design a business that is fulfilling, profitable, and sustainable. It's the antidote to feeling like you're blending into a crowded market.

- **Energetic Alignment:** When you align your business with your Human Design, you experience a natural flow, spending your time, energy, and resources intentionally while attracting opportunities that resonate with your mission. This alignment creates a magnetic presence that draws the right clients to you.

I have a client who is a 3/5 Manifestor and who has been attempting to build a business for several years as a dog trainer. She had been trying to sell eight-week training packages for a long time, yet she had struggled to get clients with the same excitement and ease she believed other local trainers had. She was forcing herself into the mold of what dog training already looked like in her community. Her Human Design described her as not only a trailblazer and an initiator of new things, but also, she was meant to do something a lot more experiential. I remember asking her, when she started my step-by-step aligned business planning program, how she felt about the repetitive programs she was promoting. "I hate them," she said. "No duh," I responded. She was perplexed. This style of repeated service was literally exhausting her even before she ever sold a package. I knew it by looking at her Human Design. She knew it because her soul was angry. This explained why she was struggling with her business. She was trying to do what she saw other people in her industry doing, but it wasn't in alignment with her Human Design. Finally, she realized that she was not a failure at business, but rather that her focus was off. She wanted to spend her energy taking clients on adventures with their dogs instead of teaching yet another dog to sit. Looking at her Human Design through the lens of business revealed that her mission was something completely different from what she had been trying to force herself to do for several years. She began to see the unique value she brought to her industry, started informing other local trainers and clients of her new path, and (spoiler) has built a more aligned, enjoyable, and successful business since then!

Using Human Design as Your Business Guide

In traditional employment, a job description outlines your role, responsibilities, and the skills needed to succeed. As a spiritual entrepreneur, you have a unique calling but might not know the specifics of your "job description." Human Design serves as that guide, helping you:

- Define your role in your business
- Understand the gifts and tools you bring to the table
- Design a business that supports your unique strengths and life purpose

Think of it this way: If you were starting a new job, you'd want to know what's expected of you and how you're best equipped to excel.

Without this clarity, you'd likely feel lost or ineffective. Your Human Design chart provides this clarity for your entrepreneurial journey, helping you step into your business with confidence and alignment.

Why Start Here?

Starting with your mission and unique value proposition ensures a strong foundation for your success. Without clarity on these, building a business can feel like throwing darts in the dark, hoping something sticks. This foundational step acts as a compass, pointing you in the right direction and ensuring that every action you take aligns with your core purpose and strengths.

Benefits of defining your mission statement and unique value proposition:

- **Avoid Distraction and Overwhelm:** As entrepreneurs, we often face an avalanche of options, strategies, and advice. Without a clear value proposition, it's easy to get pulled in multiple directions, trying to do everything and serve everyone. This approach leads to burnout and a lack of focus. Starting with your value proposition gives you a filter through which you can evaluate opportunities and decisions, helping you say yes to what aligns and no to what doesn't.

- **Set the Tone for Your Entire Business:** Your value proposition is the DNA of your business. It shapes how you design your offers, communicate with clients, and position yourself in the market. By starting here, you establish a clear vision that informs every aspect of your company, from branding to sales strategies.

- **Profitability Through Alignment:** When you're clear on your value proposition, you naturally attract the clients and opportunities that resonate with your energy. This alignment means you're working smarter, not harder, using your resources, time, energy, and money effectively. Profitability becomes a byproduct of staying true to your purpose and strengths.

- **Build Confidence and Authenticity:** Starting with your value proposition helps you understand what you bring to the table and why it matters. This self-awareness translates into confidence, which is magnetic to clients. When you're authentic and aligned, people sense it, and they're more likely to trust and invest in you.

- **Create a Long-Term Vision:** A business built on a clear value proposition is one you'll enjoy growing for years to come. Instead of chasing short-term trends or quick wins, you're focused on creating something sustainable and meaningful. This vision keeps you motivated and resilient, even when challenges arise.
- **Anchor Your Business in Purpose:** At its core, your value proposition is a reflection of your why. It's the reason you're in business, and it embodies the impact you want to create. Starting with this ensures that every decision you make aligns with your greater mission, giving you a sense of fulfillment and direction.

By creating your value proposition, you're setting the stage for a business that feels aligned, impactful, and sustainable. It's not just a step in the process; it's the foundation upon which everything else is built.

Business Elements of a Mission Statement and Unique Value Proposition

A unique value proposition is more than just a statement, it's a blueprint for how your business will operate and thrive. To craft an effective one, you need to include key components that clarify your mission, define your audience, and showcase what makes your approach unique.

1. **Your Unique Mission**
   Your mission is the cornerstone of your value proposition. What do you want to create or achieve through your business? Your mission should reflect the gap or desire you fill in the market. For example, if you're passionate about helping others heal, your mission might center on providing transformative wellness experiences that empower clients to reclaim their vitality.

Example: Our mission is to help busy professionals achieve balance and fulfillment through personalized mindfulness programs.

2. **Your Target Audience**

   Clearly identify who you serve. This includes their needs, challenges, and aspirations. The more specific you are, the easier it is to connect with your ideal clients.

   Example: We work with creative entrepreneurs who feel stuck in their growth and need strategies to scale their businesses without burnout.

3. **Your Core Offerings**

   Outline the products or services you provide to address your audience's needs. Highlight how these offerings solve their problems or meet their desires.

   Example: We offer one-on-one coaching, group workshops, and online courses to help entrepreneurs master time management and increase productivity.

4. **Your Unique Differentiation**

   What makes your approach distinct? How does your perspective, energy, or expertise make your business stand out? Your differentiation should be something your audience values and cannot easily find elsewhere.

   Example: We blend traditional business strategies with insights from Human Design, helping clients align their work with their energy for sustainable success.

5. **Your Desired Outcomes**

   What transformation or results do you promise your clients? Be clear about the benefits and value they can expect.

   Example: Our clients gain clarity, confidence, and the tools to create businesses that align with their passions and financial goals.

At the end of this chapter, there is a practical application exercise that will help you create your own mission statement and unique value proposition!

Human Design Insights to Create Your Unique Value Proposition

Your Human Design chart provides key insights into crafting your value proposition. It is more than a personality test; it is a dynamic blueprint that reveals your strengths, purpose, and unique approach to interacting with the world. Understanding how specific elements of your chart influence your business can help you build a value proposition that is truly aligned with who you are.

Incarnation Cross

The Incarnation Cross reflects your life's overarching purpose and theme. This critical aspect of your chart sheds light on what you are here to do and how you are designed to do it. Your Incarnation Cross is made up of four gates, and the specific order they are in matters. For example: My Incarnation Cross is the Left Angle Cross of Cycles (53/54 | 42/32). The four gates in the parentheses are the ones you want to pay attention to within your chart because they signify specific gifts you have been given to fulfill your purpose with the most ease.

Practical Tip: Identify these four gates in your Incarnation Cross and explore how their themes influence the work you are passionate about. You can look at my interpretations of these at my free Human Design Gates Library online at spiritualbusinessincubator.com/hdlibrary.

Profile Lines

Your Profile highlights your role in life and business. For example, a 5/1 Profile combines the practical problem-solving of the 1 with the visionary leadership of the 5, making you a magnetic leader who excels at creating innovative solutions.

Practical Tip: Align your business messaging with the strengths of your Profile. If you have a 4-Line, focus on building relationships and leveraging your network as a cornerstone of your value proposition.

Defined and Undefined Centers

Your defined centers represent areas of consistent energy and reliability, while your undefined centers show where you are open to influence and wisdom. For example, a defined Throat Center can communicate ideas powerfully, making you a natural speaker or teacher.

Practical Tip: Use the strengths of your defined centers to highlight your unique talents in your business messaging. If you have an undefined center, consider how its openness allows you to connect with clients in a meaningful way.

Gates and Channels

Gates and channels in your chart show specific energies and themes that you carry.

Practical Tip: Review the gates activated in your chart and consider how their themes can shape the services or products you offer.

Environment

Your Human Design environment describes the physical or energetic space where you thrive. For instance, if your Environment is Markets, your value proposition might focus on creating offers that feel tailored and specific to your ideal audience.

Practical Tip: Reflect on how your ideal Environment shapes your business structure and interactions. Align your work setting and client relationships to support your energetic needs.

Authority

Your Authority determines how you make aligned decisions. When integrated into your value proposition, it helps you communicate your decision-making style to clients. For example, someone with Emotional Authority might build their messaging around providing thoughtful, emotionally aware guidance.

Practical Tip: Trust your Authority in crafting offers and making decisions about your brand's direction. Explain to clients how your decision-making process ensures quality and integrity.

By getting clear on these aspects of your Human Design insights, you can create a value proposition that resonates deeply with your purpose, aligns with your strengths, and attracts the clients who are most energetically aligned with you.

Practical Application Exercise: Crafting Your Unique Value Proposition

Template Structure for a Mission Statement and Unique Value Proposition

Use the following template to craft your value proposition:

- **Mission:** I/we help [the specific audience] achieve [specific result] by [unique approach or perspective].
- **Target Audience:** I/we serve [ideal client description].
- **Core Offerings:** My/our services include [list of products/services].
- **Unique Differentiation:** What sets me/us apart is [unique quality/approach].
- **Desired Outcomes:** Clients experience [key benefits/results].

Examples

- **Mission:** We help heart-centered entrepreneurs build profitable businesses that align with their life purpose.
- **Target Audience:** Our clients are spiritual entrepreneurs, healers, teachers, guides, and leaders seeking clarity and direction in their business strategies.
- **Core Offerings:** We provide Human Design in Business readings, educational and coaching programs, self-study online courses, and interactive events.
- **Unique Differentiation:** Our approach combines practical business planning with spiritual alignment, making the process both effective and fulfilling.
- **Desired Outcomes:** Clients leave our programs with a clear business plan, feeling empowered and confident, and with aligned strategies for success.

Now put it all together!

This is an example of a unique value proposition that you would include in the beginning of your business plan in order to clearly communicate what you do or offer and how you stand out in your industry.

Example of Unique Value Proposition Combined

At the Spiritual Business Incubator™, we help mission-driven entrepreneurs build profitable businesses that align with their life purpose. Our clients are spiritual entrepreneurs, healers, teachers, guides, and leaders seeking clarity and direction in their business strategies. We provide educational and coaching programs, self-study online courses, and interactive events. Our approach combines practical business planning with spiritual alignment, making the process both effective and fulfilling. Clients leave our programs feeling empowered and confident, with a clear business plan and aligned strategies for success.

Now create yours!

Take time to draft your value proposition using the template above. Reflect on how each component aligns with your Human Design and the unique energy you bring to your business.

Common Mistakes to Avoid

- **Skipping Defining Why You Are in Business**
  Building a business without a clear understanding of your deeper purpose often results in random actions and misaligned decisions. Without your why, it's easy to get distracted by opportunities that don't support your long-term vision. Instead of chasing every trend, reflect on what truly drives you. Why did you start this business? What change do you want to create in the world? Centering your decisions around this purpose helps you stay focused and intentional.

- **Trying to Be Someone You're Not**
  One of the most common pitfalls is adopting a business model or strategy simply because it appears popular or

profitable. For example, many entrepreneurs feel pressured to offer one-on-one coaching because it's seen as a lucrative avenue, but if this format doesn't align with your natural energy or strengths, it can lead to burnout and frustration. Success comes from authenticity, not imitation. Trust your Human Design.

- **Copying Others and Acting Without Intention**
  While it's natural to draw inspiration from successful entrepreneurs, replicating someone else's strategies without considering your alignment can dilute your authenticity. Remember, your unique energy is what attracts the right clients to you. Success is not one-size-fits-all. What works for others might not work for you. Use your Human Design to create a business that feels natural and sustainable.

- **Ignoring Your Human Design**
  Misalignment often stems from ignoring your energetic blueprint. For example, Manifestors thrive on initiating and creating momentum, while Reflectors need time and space to reflect before making decisions. Building a business that conflicts with your natural rhythm can lead to stress and inconsistency. Design your schedule, offerings, and client interactions in a way that honors your energy. Aligning with your Human Design not only enhances your productivity but also ensures sustainability.

Your mission statement and unique value proposition are more than just words, they are the energetic foundation of your business. When you write this statement out, and then speak it out loud, you are effectively communicating what your business does with potential clients, partners, and collaborators. The added bonus is that you are formally declaring this to the Universe supporting the manifestation of your business to become a reality much sooner. By aligning your unique value proposition with your Human Design, you create a business that feels fulfilling, impactful, and uniquely yours. Take the time to clarify this now, and you'll build a business you love for years to come.

CHAPTER 3

CURRENT BUSINESS ASSESSMENT

The Importance of Doing a Current Business Assessment

As a visionary leader, you are driven by the excitement of what's possible. You have a powerful vision for your business, a mission that fuels you, and guiding principles that shape your decisions. But before you can confidently move forward, it's essential to pause and take an intentional assessment of exactly where you are right now. This is why doing a current business assessment is a key component of designing your aligned business blueprint.

This activity is not about going through the motions or a reason for judgment, frustration, or disappointment, it's about finding clarity, alignment, and opportunity. It is a process of objectively evaluating the current state of your business, not through an emotional lens but through awareness of the facts. When you truly understand your present situation, you gain the insight needed to make strategic, aligned decisions for the future. This chapter will guide you through this process so that you can move forward with confidence and intention.

What Is a Current Business Assessment?

This is the process of examining where your business stands in this exact moment. It is a structured, objective evaluation of the different components that make up your business, ensuring that you have a clear and honest understanding of your present reality. Here are the components involved in this process:

1. **Documenting What Your Business Looks Like at This Moment in Time**
   Before you can effectively chart the course for where you want to go, you need to establish a starting point. This assessment allows you to ground yourself in the present moment, analyzing your business from a factual, strategic perspective.

2. **Objectively Evaluating the Current State of Your Business**
   This is not an emotional exercise; it's an opportunity to gather facts. Many entrepreneurs struggle with assessing their businesses because they get caught in self-judgment or feelings of frustration over where they "should" be. However, a Current Business Assessment is about looking at things as they truly are, without attaching blame or disappointment. Objectivity is key to creating an aligned and intentional path forward.

3. **Examining Key Business Components Through the Lens of Alignment**
   Your business consists of multiple components, many of which will be outlined in this book. To ensure alignment, you must assess each component by asking yourself two fundamental questions:

   • Is this aligned with me and my unique Human Design?
   • Is this aligned with my business's Mission and Unique Value Proposition?

   By examining each area of your business with these questions in mind, you can begin to determine what is working, what isn't, and what may need to be adjusted to bring your business into full energetic and strategic alignment.

4. **Embracing This Process Without Judgment**

   This is not an exercise in self-criticism. The fact that you are taking the time to assess your current reality means that you are committing to growth and alignment. No matter what you discover in this process, remember: **Now that you know better, you can do better.** This is about gaining clarity so that you can be more intentional moving forward.

Why a Current Business Assessment Is Essential to Strategic Business Planning

In traditional business advice, you often hear that you need to stay focused on where you're going. The emphasis is always on the future: your goals, your vision, your next steps. And while that is important, not enough people are talking about the power of pausing and taking stock of where you are right now.

Here's why this step is critical:

- **Understanding Your Starting Point Allows for an Efficient Roadmap**

  If you were planning a trip, would you only focus on the destination without first knowing your current location? Of course not. Without understanding where you are starting from, mapping the journey becomes far more challenging. The same principle applies to business. By clearly assessing your present reality, you set yourself up for an efficient and effective strategy to reach your goals.

- **It Helps You Strategically Map the Path to Your Future Vision**

  Once you have a clear understanding of your business's current status, you will have the necessary foundation to create an intentional plan for achieving your "Future Business Vision" (which we will explore in the next chapter). Strategic business planning requires a deep awareness of where you are so that you can take the right next steps, rather than making decisions based on assumptions or wishful thinking.

- **It Provides Instant Clarity on What Is and Is Not in Alignment**

  When you complete this assessment, especially after exploring your Human Design from a business perspective, you will begin to see patterns emerge. Certain elements of your business will clearly feel aligned while others will stand out as misaligned or draining. This awareness empowers you to make decisions about where to invest your energy, time, and resources moving forward.

When you think of looking at your business, how does it make you feel—in your body and in your mind? When I take people through this step in my strategic business planning program, this is the part they are most anxious about because for most of them it's the first time they are looking at their business this way. The interesting thing is so many people feel bad about the way they have already built their business and think they "aren't doing it right." I had a client tell me that taking the time to look at her business this way felt like she had to look at all the things she had shoved under the bed and didn't want to deal with or look at because she thought she had done them all wrong. Have you ever felt this way?

Here's the funny thing, y'all. Of all the activities I take people through, once we are done with the Current Business Assessment, my clients say they feel like a huge weight is lifted off them. You know that feeling when you clean your house, get rid of all the old stuff you have been dragging around but haven't used for years, and see everything you need nicely organized? That is the feeling this activity creates in your business. The point of assessing your business is not to judge yourself for what you haven't done right. It's to find all the overlooked treasures and create space for what you need to grow in alignment.

Take this assessment seriously. Be honest, be objective, and remember, it's about gaining clarity not achieving perfection. Your awareness is your greatest power. Once you have completed your Current Business Assessment, you will no longer be operating on autopilot, but you may be unsure if you are moving in the right direction. You will be equipped with the awareness to make conscious, strategic, and aligned decisions for your business, ensuring that every next step is taken with clarity and confidence.

Business Elements to Assess

The goal of this section is to determine whether each component of your business is in alignment with you and your business mission.

Step 1: Objectively Document Your Business's Current State

Assess each of the following areas and why they matter:

- **Current Clients:** Who are you currently serving? Do they align with your ideal client profile? Are these the people you want to work with long-term?
- **Business Model:** How are you structured? Is this model sustainable and fulfilling? Does it provide you with financial stability and work-life balance?
- **Services and Offers:** Are these services aligned with your strengths, passions, and audience needs? How do you want to structure your offers to maximize your skills and meet your clients' needs efficiently?
- **Marketing Pathways:** Which marketing efforts are bringing in leads? Are they effective and enjoyable? Are you using the right strategies for your business type and Human Design?
- **Sales Process:** How do you attract, nurture, and convert leads into clients? Is it working? Does your process feel natural and aligned with your values?
- **Client Journey:** What is the full experience from discovery to completion of service? Are your clients receiving the transformation you promised?
- **Operations Structure (Team and Systems):** What systems and support do you have in place? Are they efficient? Are you handling too much on your own? Do you have the right team and automation in place, or could you use improvement?

- **Resources: Time, Energy, Money:** Where are your resources being spent? Are they yielding results? Are you overextending yourself in areas that don't bring ROI?

Step 2: Assess What's Working and What's Not

Compare your current reality to your Mission and Unique Value Proposition. Consider these:

- **Practical Alignment:** What activities are actually helping the business grow?
- **Enjoyment Alignment:** Are you excited about what you do every day? How do you feel when you think about doing this activity going forward?

This clarity will help you decide what to keep, adjust, or remove as you build a more aligned business structure.

Human Design Elements to Help Assess Alignment

Your Human Design provides valuable insights into whether you are in alignment or operating from a Not-Self place. When you build a business that aligns with your natural energy, decision-making process, and strategy for engagement, you create a foundation for sustainable success. Below, we explore key Human Design elements that influence business alignment and how you can use them to refine your business approach.

Signature Versus Not-Self Themes

Each Human Design Type has a **Signature Theme**, which signals alignment and flow, and a **Not-Self Theme**, which indicates resistance and frustration. Recognizing these themes in your business allows you to make adjustments that keep you aligned with your natural energy flow.

- **Manifestor:** Alignment feels like *peace*, while misalignment leads to *anger*. A Manifestor in alignment initiates powerfully and effortlessly, whereas one out of alignment struggles with resistance and burnout.

- **Projector:** Alignment brings *success*, while misalignment results in *bitterness*. A Projector thrives when recognized for their wisdom and works efficiently rather than hustling.
- **Generator:** Alignment brings *satisfaction*, while misalignment leads to frustration. Generators excel when engaging in work they deeply enjoy rather than forcing themselves into roles that feel draining.
- **Manifesting Generator:** Alignment is a mix of *satisfaction and excitement*, while misalignment results in *frustration and anger*. MGs need variety and efficiency in their work rather than strict, rigid structures.
- **Reflector:** Alignment feels like *surprise and delight*, while misalignment brings *disappointment*. Reflectors thrive in environments that allow them to sample and reflect before committing.

By understanding these themes, you can assess which aspects of your business make you feel aligned and which create resistance, helping you refine your business strategy accordingly.

Using Your Strategy and Authority to Assess Your Business

Your **Strategy** determines how you best engage with opportunities, and your **Authority** is your unique decision-making mechanism. Both are crucial for making aligned business decisions. Important note: Strategy and Authority are intended to be used together, like two partners dancing in sync. Understanding how your rhythm looks and feels is an important part of your Human Design exploration, especially if you are making decisions and taking action in business.

Strategies

- **Manifestors – To Inform:** Manifestors thrive when they initiate action and inform others of their direction. In business, this means launching new ideas, products, or services without waiting for permission. A Manifestor entrepreneur might create a new course and announce it boldly to their audience before executing it, ensuring alignment and reducing resistance.

- **Generators and Manifesting Generators – Wait to Respond:** These Types must engage with opportunities that naturally present themselves. A Generator coach might receive repeated inquiries about a specific type of service and realize this is the right path to focus on. Manifesting Generators, on the other hand, may need multiple projects running at once, ensuring they are engaging with what excites them most.

- **Projectors – Wait for the Invitation:** Projectors excel when they position themselves as guides and wait for recognition. A Projector business consultant might create high-value content showcasing their expertise and allow invitations to consult to arise naturally rather than chasing leads.

- **Reflectors – Wait a Lunar Cycle:** Reflectors need time to assess major decisions, so a Reflector business owner considering a new partnership might observe interactions, collect feedback, and wait a full lunar cycle before making a commitment.

Authorities

Each Authority represents the best way for you to make business decisions:

- **Emotional (Solar Plexus):** Decisions should not be made in the heat of the moment. A business owner with Emotional Authority might receive an exciting collaboration offer but will wait a few days to ensure clarity before committing.

- **Sacral:** The gut response is key. A Generator with Sacral Authority deciding on a new business direction will check in with their body, and if they feel energized and excited, they proceed; if they feel drained or uncertain, they step back.

- **Splenic:** This Authority requires trusting intuitive hits. A Splenic entrepreneur might sense immediately that a networking event will be beneficial and act on that instinct without second-guessing.

- **Ego Manifested:** Following desires and vocal expression is key. A Manifestor with this Authority might feel a strong personal drive toward a project and verbalize their excitement, ensuring it's aligned before proceeding.

- **Self-Projected:** Speaking decisions aloud helps clarify alignment. A Self-Projected Projector might talk through business ideas with a mentor or friend, realizing which option resonates most as they speak.
- **Ego Projected:** Decision-making is based on personal willpower and heart-driven goals. This Authority means a business owner might only take on projects that deeply resonate with their values and self-worth.
- **Mental (Environment):** External perspectives and surroundings influence decisions. A Mental Projector making a business shift might consult with trusted advisors and ensure they are in a supportive environment before finalizing choices.
- **Lunar:** Time and observation are essential. A Reflector considering launching a new offer will take a month to consider, ensuring it truly aligns with their energy before proceeding.

Understanding your Strategy and Authority enables you to make business decisions with ease and confidence, reducing resistance and improving alignment with your true self.

Practical Application Exercise: Setting Intention

Take a moment to intentionally think high level about your business. Set the intention that you are going to explore your business both from a practical/objective perspective and from a Human Design alignment perspective.

1. Get out two pieces of paper—
   a. On one, write Working / In Alignment.
   b. On the other, write Not Working / Not in Alignment.
   c. Sit in a reflective state and brain dump as much as you can on each of these pages.

2. Now compare the things on both lists with your mission and unique value proposition.

    a. First look at these and feel into the emotions around them. It is important to be emotionally connected to what you are creating.

    b. Make objective assessments on whether the things you wrote on both pages are actually helping you meet your business mission.

3. Use your signature and Not-Self themes to help decide if each thing is aligned, not aligned, or unsure.

    a. If aligned, know you can/will incorporate this into your business plan.

    b. If not aligned, determine whether it needs to be stopped completely or modified.

    c. If unsure, this likely means you need to think more deeply about the activity or gather more information.

4. Reflection Questions

    a. What activities in my current business are fully in alignment with the overall mission of my business?

    b. What activities am I trying to force even though they are not aligned with my business mission?

Common Mistakes to Avoid

Assessing your business is a crucial step in identifying opportunities for growth and alignment, but many visionary entrepreneurs unknowingly make mistakes that limit the effectiveness of this process. Here are three common missteps to watch out for:

- **Focusing Too Much on the Future Without an Honest Look at the Present**
  Visionary entrepreneurs tend to be forward-thinking, often more focused on where they want to go rather than where they currently are. While vision is essential, skipping over an honest assessment of your current strengths, weaknesses, and business performance can lead to misaligned strategies. The key is to balance your long-term vision with a realistic understanding of your present foundation.

- **Evaluating the Business Solely from a Financial Perspective**
Many entrepreneurs judge their success based on revenue alone, overlooking other critical factors like fulfillment, workflow efficiency, audience engagement, and energetic alignment. While financial health is important, a truly sustainable and aligned business thrives when all aspects (such as client experience, team dynamics, and personal well-being) are assessed holistically.

- **Ignoring Misalignment in Offers and Business Structure**
It's easy to hold onto offers, strategies, or business models that once worked but no longer feel aligned or that are no longer meeting the future vision of the business. Entrepreneurs often resist change due to fear of doing it differently, upsetting clients, and imagining the work involved to evolve. However, during a current business assessment is the perfect time to evaluate whether your offers and business model still reflect your strengths, values, and Human Design. If something feels off, it's a prime opportunity to evolve in a way that better supports your energy and long-term vision.

Avoiding these common mistakes ensures your business assessment provides real clarity, empowering you to make aligned decisions that support your vision, impact, and sustainable success.

CHAPTER 4

CRAFTING YOUR BUSINESS MISSION AND FUTURE VISION

The Power of a Clear Business Mission

Your business mission is the guiding force behind everything you create and build. It is the foundational statement that explains why your business exists and what impact you are here to make in the world. As a visionary leader, you are not just running a business, you are fulfilling a calling, a purpose that is uniquely yours.

What Is Your Business Mission?

At its core, your business mission is the overarching umbrella that defines the purpose of your business. It is not just about what you do but also about the transformation you bring to others and the greater vision you hold for the world.

1. **Definition:** Your mission articulates the deeper *reason* for your business's existence beyond just making money. It's the energetic and strategic anchor that keeps you focused.

2. **The Vehicle for Impact:** Your business is more than just a source of income, it is a vehicle for change, a way to contribute to the collective in a way that is uniquely aligned with your energy and purpose.

3. **The Power of Intentionality:** Sustainable, fulfilling, and profitable success in business starts with clarity. When you are clear on your mission, your decisions become more intentional, aligned with your Human Design, and structured to support the bigger picture of your vision.

4. **Life and Business as One:** Many spiritual entrepreneurs find that their life and business blend together, and their mission is intertwined with their personal purpose. This differs from traditional entrepreneurs who may build businesses solely for profit. Without a clear mission, businesses tend to operate reactively, which leads to inefficiencies.

What Is Your Personal Future Vision?

Many people embark on the entrepreneurial journey because they want to make a positive impact and create a better life for themselves and their loved ones. However, few take the time to deeply define what this future vision actually looks like. Without clarity, entrepreneurs often get caught in comparison traps, chasing business models that don't actually align with their true desires.

1. **Entrepreneurial Intentions:** Business owners often start with the dream of freedom, impact, and financial success, but without clearly defining what that looks like, they risk straying from their own authentic path.

2. **Comparison Creates Confusion:** Without a clear vision, it's easy to be distracted by what others are doing, leading to decisions based on external influences rather than personal alignment.

3. **Business Model Versus Lifestyle Fit:** One of the most common misalignments I see is entrepreneurs building businesses that do not align with their ideal lifestyle. Your

business structure should support your life vision, not work against it.

4. **The Energy of Self-Sacrifice:** Many entrepreneurs operate from a subconscious programming that equates success with struggle. However, true service does not require personal sacrifice; when you take care of yourself first, your impact multiplies.

5. **Solution:** To prevent burnout, you must align your business vision with your personal happiness, health, and long-term sustainability. Ask yourself:

   • What does a balanced and fulfilling life look like to me?
   • What kind of legacy do I want to build for my family, my community?
   • How can my business fuel both my personal and professional growth?

Why You Need to Explicitly Define Your Mission and Vision

Having a clearly defined mission and future vision is essential for:

1. **Maintaining Focus:** It serves as a North Star, helping you measure whether your daily, weekly, and yearly decisions are in alignment with your larger purpose.

2. **Using Resources Wisely:** Your time, energy, and money should be directed toward strategic growth rather than scattered efforts that lead to wasted resources.

3. **Creating Sustainable Success:** Without clear intentions, entrepreneurs often chase trends instead of building something deeply fulfilling and long-lasting.

Business Elements You Need to Define

Mission and Vision Statement

A well-defined mission statement is a *public declaration* of what you do and how you serve.

- **Who You Serve:** Define your ideal clients/customers and their transformation.
- **How You Serve:** Clearly articulate what your business provides.
- **Inspiration and Aspiration:** Your statement should be motivational and impact driven.

Core Values and Guiding Principles

Your values are the *foundational beliefs* that drive your decisions in business. These act as a compass for:

- How you create and structure offers
- Your approach to marketing and sales
- The way you interact with clients and partners

Having three to five clear values make decision-making faster and easier, eliminating doubt and wasted energy.

Human Design Elements to Help You Write Your Mission Statement

Your Human Design provides a unique and highly personalized perspective on defining your business mission and future vision. By integrating these elements into your mission statement, you can create a business that aligns with your natural strengths and highest purpose. Let's explore how each Human Design component can help craft a more aligned and effective mission statement, along with practical applications.

Incarnation Cross (a.k.a. Your Life Purpose)

Your **Incarnation Cross** (IC) represents your overarching life purpose and the impact you are meant to make in the world. This is one of the most important elements to consider when defining your business mission.

The Cross Category

- **Right Angle Cross (Personal Karma):** If you have a Right Angle Cross, your mission is deeply personal and focused on your own experience. You are here to fulfill your purpose for yourself first, and by doing so, you naturally inspire and lead others. Your business mission will likely reflect your *own transformational story*, making your personal experiences a key aspect of your brand. For example, a business coach with a Right Angle Cross might say: "I help ambitious entrepreneurs align with their true calling by sharing the strategies that transformed my own career."

- **Left Angle Cross (Transpersonal Karma):** A Left Angle Cross means your purpose is tied to *helping others evolve.* You are designed to work with people, share wisdom, and facilitate transformation. Your business mission will likely have a strong *interpersonal* component, whether through mentoring, coaching, or community building. A therapist or leadership consultant with a Left Angle Cross might craft a mission like: "I facilitate workshops for high-performing professionals to create sustainable success by understanding their unique strengths."

- **Juxtaposed Cross (Fixed Fate):** If you have a Juxtaposed Cross, your mission is *stable and consistent*, meaning you hold a unique role in bridging personal and collective transformation. Your business mission might focus on *offering structured and lasting solutions*, allowing you to create something that continues to impact people for generations. A business strategist with a Juxtaposed Cross could say: "I provide entrepreneurs with proven frameworks to build businesses that stand the test of time."

Incarnation Cross Gates

The four gates in your Incarnation Cross (which are ordered Personality Sun, Personality Earth, Design Sun, and Design Earth) form the foundation of your life's purpose and, therefore, the mission of your business. Each of these gates represents a unique energy that influences how you express yourself and the work you are here to do.

- **Personality Sun:** This gate is your highest conscious expression (a.k.a. Highest Gift), the primary energy you radiate into the world. It represents the *primary core strength* of your business mission and should be highlighted in your messaging.

- **Personality Earth:** This gate represents *what grounds you* and provides stability. It is the balancing force for your Personality Sun, ensuring that you stay aligned with your purpose.
- **Design Sun:** This gate is your *unconscious life purpose*, the energy you are designed to express, even if you don't always recognize it. It reveals an innate strength that fuels your business.
- **Design Earth:** This gate provides the *deep internal stability* that keeps you aligned and prevents burnout. It ensures that your business mission remains sustainable.

How to infuse these gates into your mission statement:

- **Shadow to Gift Spectrum:** Understanding the shadow and gift aspects of this gate helps you recognize when you're in alignment and when you may be out of alignment. Not only are you moving from shadow to the gift energy of these gates, but also you are leading your clients through this.
- **Entrepreneur Perspective:** How do you use this energy in your business offerings, leadership style, or content? When you look at the definitions of these gates, how do they practically apply to how you want to be seen in your industry?
- **Client Perspective:** How does this energy serve your audience and provide transformation? Ultimately, you are here to serve a client but the best way for you to do this is by doing so in alignment with your gifts. How does the gift energy of these gates support your clients in a unique way?

Consider the Quarter

The quarter in which your Incarnation Cross is located provides deeper insight into the overarching theme that influences your life's purpose and, consequently, your business mission. Each of the four quarters represents a distinct energetic focus, shaping how you express your purpose through your work.

- **Quarter of Initiation (Mind):** This quarter is about mental expansion, wisdom, and sharing knowledge. If your Incarnation Cross is in this quarter, your business mission will likely focus on *teaching, guiding, and helping others shift their perspectives*. You might create content-driven businesses such as coaching, thought leadership, or writing books to share transformative insights.

Example: A mindset coach whose mission is to help entrepreneurs overcome limiting beliefs through education and perspective shifts.

- **Quarter of Civilization (Manifestation and Structure):** This quarter is about bringing ideas into tangible form and creating structures that support life. If your Incarnation Cross falls here, your business mission will likely involve *building, organizing, and bringing practical solutions into reality*. You may thrive in creating frameworks, systems, or tools that help people manifest their goals effectively.

  Example: A business strategist whose mission is to provide sustainable systems that help entrepreneurs scale their businesses with ease.

- **Quarter of Duality (Relationships and Connection):** This quarter focuses on relationships, interaction, and deep connection with others. If your Incarnation Cross is in this quarter, your business mission will likely center on *collaboration, emotional intelligence, and community-building*. Your work may focus on fostering authentic connections, healing relationships, or creating spaces where people feel supported.

  Example: A relationship coach whose mission is to help couples deepen their connection and improve communication for lasting harmony.

- **Quarter of Mutation (Transformation and Change):** This quarter is about innovating, evolving, and bringing new paradigms into existence. If your Incarnation Cross is here, your business mission will likely revolve around *transformation, disruption, and pioneering new ways of thinking*. You may naturally challenge norms and introduce innovative solutions that change industries or societal structures.

Example: A tech entrepreneur whose mission is to disrupt outdated business models and introduce cutting-edge technology for a new era of business growth.

Understanding the quarter of your Incarnation Cross helps ensure your business mission aligns with the natural energy you are meant to express, making your work both fulfilling and impactful.

Profile (Your Business Role)

Your Profile in Human Design represents the unique way you interact with the world, how you are naturally wired to lead in your business, and how others perceive and receive you. It is made up of two numbers, each with a distinct influence on your entrepreneurial journey.

- **The First Number (Conscious Identity):** This is the part of your profile that you are *aware of* and embody in your day-to-day life. It reflects how you *naturally show up* in business and what people are actively seeking from you.
- **The Second Number (Unconscious Identity):** This is the *deeper, subconscious* part of you that influences your actions in ways you may not always recognize. To fully express the potential of your conscious identity, you must embrace and integrate this part of your profile.

For example, if someone has a 5/1 Profile, their 5 (conscious) is the visionary problem-solver that people look to for leadership and practical solutions, while their 1 (unconscious) means they have a deep need for research and a solid foundation to feel confident in their leadership role. Understanding this balance allows them to build a business that fully supports their strengths.

The 12 Profile Combinations and Their Entrepreneurial Impact

Understanding your Human Design Profile is one of the most important influences in your business. It impacts who you are as the business owner, how you are meant to stand out to attract clients, the business model and services you choose to deliver, the way you market, and the way you sell. All of it. Yet, I have always found the traditional descriptions given for the Profile Lines and the combinations to be hard to understand in the context of entrepreneurship. Thus, I have renamed these from an entrepreneurial lens, and you can get the full descriptions when you order your Entrepreneur by Design report at spiritualbusinessincubator.com/business-report. For the context of this book, here are some short descriptions of how your business mission is impacted by your Profile.

Profile 1/3

Traditional Identity: Investigator/Martyr

Entrepreneur Identity: The Insightful Experimenter

- **Mission:** To master knowledge through research and experimentation before sharing insights with the world.
- **Entrepreneurial Role:** These entrepreneurs are deep researchers who master their craft through knowledge and hands-on experience. Their business mission is about discovering and testing new methods before sharing them with others.
- **Examples:**
  - A business strategist who extensively researches marketing techniques, implements them, and then shares the most effective ones through courses and consulting.
  - A spiritual teacher who studies multiple energy healing modalities, experiments with their effectiveness, and then creates a comprehensive healing method to share with clients.

Profile 1/4

Traditional Identity: Investigator/Opportunist

Entrepreneur Identity: The Insightful Connector

- **Mission:** To establish a solid foundation of knowledge and share it through trusted relationships and community.
- **Entrepreneurial Role:** They succeed when they balance deep expertise with relationship-building, often excelling in mentorship, coaching, or advisory roles.
- **Examples:**
  - A financial planner who provides clients with well-researched investment strategies and gains trust through personal referrals.
  - A psychic and Akashic Records guide who studies these extensively and creates a close-knit membership community to share and deepen understanding with others.

Profile 2/4

Traditional Identity: Hermit/Opportunist

Entrepreneur Identity: The Intuitive Connector

- **Mission:** To leverage innate talents while relying on organic relationships to expand influence. Their mission revolves around *effortless expertise and connecting* with the right people.
- **Entrepreneurial Role:** They thrive when operating in a way that feels natural and are often sought out by others for their gifts. They succeed by embracing their *natural gifts* and fostering meaningful relationships.
- **Examples:**
  - A brand designer who effortlessly creates compelling visuals and attracts clients through word-of-mouth and personal recommendations.
  - A Reiki healer who naturally attracts clients and builds their business through word-of-mouth referrals and heartfelt connections.

Profile 2/5

Traditional Identity: Hermit/Heretic

Entrepreneur Identity: The Intuitive Pathfinder

- **Mission:** To embrace natural abilities while being seen as a solution provider for others.
- **Entrepreneurial Role:** People come to them for answers, so they often excel in consulting, leadership, or transformational coaching. These entrepreneurs have an *innate genius* and an ability to step into leadership when people need solutions.
- **Examples:**
  - A health coach who intuitively understands how to help people transform their well-being and becomes a sought-after expert in holistic wellness.
  - A shadow work coach who has an innate gift for identifying patterns in clients and guiding them to breakthrough realizations.

Profile 3/5

Traditional Identity: Martyr /Heretic

Entrepreneur Identity: The Experimental Pathfinder

- **Mission:** To discover new ways of doing things through personal trial and error and share solutions with others. Their business mission is about *transformation through lived experience.*
- **Entrepreneurial Role:** These entrepreneurs are highly adaptive and become industry changemakers by refining broken systems. They *learn through trial and error* and bring innovative solutions to others.
- **Examples:**
  - A tech entrepreneur who experiments with innovative software solutions, learns from failures, and launches groundbreaking products.

- A somatic coach who has experimented with multiple nervous system regulating techniques and now teaches others what truly works.

Profile 3/6

Traditional Identity: Martyr/Role Model

Entrepreneur Identity: The Experimental Advisor

- **Mission:** To go through personal transformations that allow them to become an authority figure in their field.
- **Entrepreneurial Role:** They go through phases of deep learning, eventually becoming trusted mentors and role models for others. They become industry leaders through lived experience, eventually stepping into mentorship roles.
- **Examples:**
  - A mindset coach who overcame personal struggles and now guides others through the same transformation.
  - An energy healer who initially explored different modalities before becoming a recognized teacher and mentor.

Profile 4/6

Traditional Identity: Opportunist/Role Model

Entrepreneur Identity: The Influential Advisor

- **Mission:** To create meaningful connections while gradually stepping into a leadership role as a trusted expert. Their business mission is about building community and leading by example.
- **Entrepreneurial Role:** They are natural community builders who become respected authorities through their network. They are influential connectors who eventually become trusted mentors.

- **Examples:**
  - A leadership trainer who first gains influence through strong relationships and later establishes themself as a keynote speaker.
  - A spiritual retreat leader who builds a high-vibration community and facilitates deep, collective healing experiences.

Profile 4/1

Traditional Identity: Opportunist/Investigator

Entrepreneur Identity: The Influential Expert

- **Mission:** To build strong relationships while establishing a deep knowledge base that supports their work.
- **Entrepreneurial Role:** They thrive by building strong relationships while grounding their expertise in deep knowledge. They naturally gather and distribute information in structured ways, excelling in content creation, training, and strategic consulting.
- **Examples:**
  - A thought leader who writes extensively researched books and gains credibility through networking events.
  - A tarot expert who teaches a structured, research-based approach to intuitive readings within a devoted student community.

Profile 5/1

Traditional Identity: Heretic /Investigator

Entrepreneur Identity: The Trailblazing Expert

- **Mission:** To offer practical and innovative solutions backed by a strong foundation of knowledge.
- **Entrepreneurial Role:** These individuals are problem-solvers that people naturally seek out for guidance. They are designed to step into leadership positions and guide others through structured expertise.

- **Examples:**
  - A business consultant who crafts powerful systems and frameworks to help businesses scale effectively.
  - A Human Design coach who builds a structured coaching certification program to train other practitioners.

Profile 5/2

Traditional Identity: Heretic/Hermit

Entrepreneur Identity: The Trailblazing Visionary

- **Mission:** To be an impactful leader who delivers innovative solutions in a way that feels effortless.
- **Entrepreneurial Role:** They are natural leaders who bring impactful solutions in a way that feels effortless to them but revolutionary to others. They are seen as trusted problem-solvers, often leading movements or revolutionary change in their industry.
- **Examples:**
  - A transformational coach who intuitively leads clients to breakthroughs while working in a way that aligns with their natural rhythm.
  - A spiritual business mentor who intuitively creates aligned strategies that help other spiritual entrepreneurs scale their impact.

Profile 6/2

Traditional Identity: Role Model/Hermit

Entrepreneur Identity: The Enlightened Visionary

- **Mission:** To experience different phases of growth before becoming a highly respected mentor.
- **Entrepreneurial Role:** They move through three life phases: experimentation, retreat, and mentorship—ultimately serving as role models.

- **Examples:**
  - A feminine energetics coach who first goes through personal evolution before becoming a sought-after mentor and speaker.
  - A meditation teacher who first explores deep personal stillness before becoming a sought-after master instructor.

Profile 6/3

Traditional Identity: Role Model/Martyr

Entrepreneur Identity: The Enlightened Experimenter

- **Mission:** To go through lifelong cycles of transformation and share wisdom through experiential learning.
- **Entrepreneurial Role:** They transition through stages of growth, eventually becoming wise and trusted mentors. These individuals thrive when they embrace change and guide others through uncertainty.
- **Examples:**
  - A life coach who constantly reinvents their approach based on new experiences, inspiring clients to embrace transformation in their own lives.
  - A shamanic practitioner who undergoes deep, personal initiations and later facilitates transformational experiences for clients.

How to Craft Your Mission Statement

1. **Embrace Your Profile:** What strengths and skills do people naturally seek from you? What do you need to cultivate within yourself to step into your best entrepreneurial role?
2. **Align with Your Incarnation Cross:** This is your life purpose and the driving force of the work you do in this lifetime. Ask yourself: How does this align with the business I am trying to create and the people I am trying to serve?
3. **Combine These to Craft Your Mission Statement:** Build a mission that supports your unique way of leading and serving.

By understanding and leveraging your Profile, you can *craft a business mission statement that fully embodies your natural strengths*, ensuring an authentic, impactful, and sustainable business model. Your Profile determines how you naturally interact with the world and the role you play in your business. Understanding this allows you to craft a mission that highlights your strengths and leadership style.

Practical Application Exercise: Writing an Aligned Mission Statement

Your mission statement is a reflection of your purpose and the impact you want to create in the world. Using your Human Design as a guide, you can craft a mission statement that feels deeply aligned, authentic, and sustainable. This approach goes beyond using generic business templates and instead focuses on drawing from your unique energy, gifts, and role. Follow these steps to leverage your Human Design in writing your mission statement.

1. **Reflect on Your Incarnation Cross:** Your Incarnation Cross provides key insights into the overarching themes of your purpose. What recurring themes or patterns define your role in life and business? Consider how these themes can inform the impact you want to make through your business.

2. **Identify Your Conscious Sun Gift:** Your Conscious Sun represents your greatest strength and area of self-expression. Ask yourself how you can use this gift to serve others. What qualities or skills come naturally to you, and how can these strengths shine through in your mission statement?

3. **Consider Your Profile:** Your Human Design Profile reveals the role you naturally play in your business and how you interact with others. Are you a trailblazing leader, a natural collaborator, or someone who excels in teaching and guiding others? Understanding your role helps ensure that your mission aligns with how you're meant to show up in the world.

4. **Combine These Insights:** Use the themes from your Incarnation Cross, the strengths of your Conscious Sun, and the natural role of your Profile to craft a mission statement that

feels aligned and authentic. Your mission should reflect who you are and the impact you're meant to create through your business.

Your Human Design offers a unique lens for defining your mission and vision, helping you create a foundation that feels aligned and purposeful. One powerful step in this process is to write down three to five core values. These values act as guiding principles for your mission, vision, and day-to-day decisions, ensuring that your business remains rooted in its true purpose even as it grows and evolves. By anchoring yourself in these values, you create a compass that keeps your business direction clear and aligned with who you are.

By approaching your mission statement from this perspective, you can ensure that it embodies your natural energy and supports you in creating a business that is powerful, purposeful, and truly aligned with who you are.

Common Mistakes to Avoid

1. **Focusing Only on Business Without Considering Personal Fulfillment:** Many entrepreneurs craft business plans without considering how their personal goals and desired lifestyle align with their business model. This often leads to burnout and resentment toward their work. Instead, integrate your personal vision with your business goals to create a holistic approach.

2. **Thinking Too Small and Minimizing Potential Impact:** Your business mission should inspire and energize you. If it doesn't feel expansive or exciting, you may be limiting yourself. Allow yourself to dream big, trusting that the right systems, support, and opportunities will arise as you take aligned action.

3. **Chasing Only Money Instead of Impact:** Prioritizing financial success over aligned service can lead to frustration and dissatisfaction. When you focus on fulfilling your true mission and bringing genuine value to your audience, financial abundance will follow as a byproduct of your service.

By defining your mission and vision with clarity and alignment, you create a business that is both profitable and fulfilling. This is the foundation for long-term success and a purpose-driven business that feels authentic to you.

CHAPTER 5
DEFINING YOUR NICHE

What Is a Niche?

A niche refers to the specific group of people you serve and the unique problem you solve for them. In traditional business terms, a niche is defined as a specialized segment of the market. For many visionary entrepreneurs, defining a niche feels overwhelming. In a practical business sense, it is all about consciously choosing a segment of the market or industry. From a soul perspective, it is about aligning your work with your soul's calling. From a Human Design perspective, it is all about aligning with the people you are energetically designed to serve. This combination I believe is the easiest path to help the right people recognize the value of your work.

Understanding the Business Definition of a Niche

A niche can be determined in multiple ways.

- **A specific group of people:** These could be individuals who share common characteristics, values, interests, or experiences.

- **A specific solution you provide or desire you fulfill:** Your niche may revolve around solving a problem, alleviating pain points, or fulfilling a specific need.
- **A combination of both:** The most aligned and effective niches incorporate both a clearly defined audience and a unique solution tailored to them.

In essence, your niche is either the person you serve, the problem you solve, the desire you fulfill, or a blend of all three. The best-case scenario is when you can define both the *who* (the people you serve) and the *what* (the transformation or solution you offer).

The Human Design Perspective: Your Fractal Line

From a Human Design perspective, the people you are designed to serve are part of your **Fractal Line**, a concept that refers to the cosmic connections between you and those you are naturally meant to help. These are the clients, relationships, and opportunities that feel synchronistic and aligned. Your fractal clients are often described as soulmate clients, the ones who deeply resonate with your work and benefit from it on a profound level.

When you are clear on your Fractal Line, you stop trying to convince people of your value. Instead, you naturally attract the right people, those who recognize your worth and are eager to work with you.

The Common Struggle: Getting Stuck in Niche Selection

Many entrepreneurs struggle with choosing a niche because they fear making the wrong decision. Some worry that narrowing their focus will limit opportunities, while others overthink the process and stay in analysis paralysis. But the truth is this:

- **You get to choose your niche.** Who are you called to serve? How are you called to serve? What characteristics define these people?

- **Your niche can include multiple factors.** It may be based on demographics, psychographics, shared experiences, Human Design elements, or a combination of these.
- **Market research helps validate your niche.** Understanding your audience's needs, challenges, and willingness to invest in your services ensures that your niche is both aligned and profitable.

The Power of Clarity in Your Niche

When you gain clarity on your niche, you unlock multiple business advantages.

- You confidently position yourself in the market and differentiate yourself from others.
- Your business model, offers, and messaging become clearer and more strategic.
- You make more aligned decisions about marketing, sales, and visibility.
- You ensure that your niche is not just fulfilling but also aligned with your long-term business goals and personal aspirations.

The Cost of Not Having Clarity

Without a clearly defined niche, entrepreneurs often struggle with:

- generic or ineffective messaging that fails to attract the right people,
- misaligned marketing efforts, positioning themselves in the wrong places, and
- wasted time and energy trying to serve an audience that doesn't resonate.

A Personal Example: Finding My Niche

When I first started my business, I attended local networking events through my Chamber of Commerce in my rural, conservative town in Colorado. I quickly realized that most people there had never heard of Human Design, let alone believed in it as a viable business tool. This experience forced me to ask myself:

- Should I focus my efforts on educating people about Human Design from the ground up?
- Or should I direct my energy toward serving spiritual entrepreneurs who already understand and love Human Design?

Choosing the latter allowed me to position my business in front of people who were already aligned with my work. Instead of trying to convince people of its value, I focused on helping those who already recognized it, allowing my business to grow with ease and alignment.

Not Everyone Is Meant to Be Your Client (and That's a Good Thing)

A common mistake entrepreneurs make is trying to serve everyone. Even if you believe your services could help a broad range of people, not everyone will value your work enough to invest in it.

Some key truths to remember:

- Your ideal client must desire the transformation you offer and be willing to exchange value for it. Otherwise, you could feel like you are convincing people that what you offer is valuable. The goal is to choose a niche you can serve that already finds value in what you deliver, so then your focus is on building relationships and differentiating your business in the market.
- Not everyone who *could* benefit from your work is meant to be in your niche. This is ultimately rooted in awareness and personal choice. Some people are not yet ready to receive what you have to offer because of their own mindset and beliefs around what you do. Other people may simply not yet be ready to prioritize your solution enough to pay for it. This is not a reflection on your ability to deliver and serve.
- Defining your niche allows you to attract aligned clients and create a thriving, sustainable business. Often times when entrepreneurs are struggling to define a niche, they change directions frequently, which actually creates doubt in the market of

their ability to deliver and serve. Every time you change your niche, there is a negative trickle-down effect on your business, and you are often starting over and over without building long-term sustainability in your business. By doing the work to intentionally choose a niche that aligns with you personally, meets your business vision, and is viable in the market, you are setting yourself and your clients up for more positive outcomes.

Many different approaches exist for identifying niche, and there is no one-size-fits-all formula. However, gaining clarity on yours is one of the most important steps in building an aligned, profitable business. The sooner you define who you are meant to serve, the sooner you can start making an impact.

The Business Element of Finding Your Niche

Identifying your ideal client requires market research, not assumptions. Many entrepreneurs create an imaginary client without real-world validation, leading to ineffective marketing and unclear messaging. And still others are taught that their ideal client is a past version of themselves, which is not true for all people and businesses. Instead, you need to conduct market research and intentionally analyze trends and make conscious decisions on who you want to serve with your business.

- Who naturally engages with your work?
- What common struggles do they share?
- What transformations have past clients experienced?

You Get to Choose Who You Serve

You are not bound to a niche that chooses you; you actively choose the niche that aligns with your passion, expertise, and long-term vision. If you feel called to serve a particular audience, trust that intuition, but validate it with research. A clear decision about your niche boosts confidence and creates a ripple effect throughout your business, making every other strategic decision easier.

Market Research Needs to Be Ongoing

Market research helps you identify *gaps in the market* and ensures that your offers meet actual demand. There are two primary approaches.

- **Structured:** Surveys, polls, interviews.
- **Casual:** Social media engagement, client conversations, industry trend analysis.

Continually analyzing market trends, competitor positioning, and evolving client needs allows you to refine your niche over time. Testing new offers and gathering feedback ensures that you adjust based on actual demand rather than assumptions.

Market Positioning to Attract Your Aligned Niche

Once you define your niche, you can intentionally position yourself to attract high-quality clients. This requires the following:

- Aligning your messaging so it resonates with your ideal audience
- Evaluating your current audience to see if they reflect your desired niche
- Shifting your communication strategy—if needed—to attract more aligned prospects
- Meeting your clients where they are, whether online or in-person
- Positioning yourself as an authority by producing valuable content and maintaining a clear and consistent message

The Human Design Elements to Give You Niche Clarity

Finding clarity in your niche is about more than just identifying a target market, it's about aligning your work with your natural strengths, energy, and purpose. This is where Human Design becomes an invaluable tool for visionary entrepreneurs. Instead of choosing a niche based on external trends or what seems profitable, your Human

Design reveals how you are naturally designed to lead, communicate, and serve.

Your Personality Sun and the People You Serve

Your Personality Sun or Conscious Sun in Human Design reveals your highest gift, making up 70 percent of your energy, specifically so you can use this gift to fulfill your Incarnation Cross. It's something that when you consciously reflect on your life, comes completely naturally to you. All the gates have a spectrum of their frequency, from low expression (also called shadow) to high expression (called gift).

The way I explain this in my programs is that you have this highest gift so you can give it to the world. That means that there are people out there who don't have this gate defined in their chart or maybe have it defined but are experiencing the low/shadow expression of this gate. What does this mean for your niche? It means that your ideal clients are naturally drawn to you because they lack what you inherently embody. They are energetically drawn to you because of this gift.

Thus, when you understand that people are attracted to you for this reason, you can start looking at the shadow or low expression qualities of this gate to more clearly define the challenges that your aligned clients are currently experiencing

Understanding this helps you identify who needs your work the most.

Take some time to look at your Personality Sun Gate in more depth. Read about this gate from several different sources. If you have purchased a personalized Human Design for Business report from my site, you will see that it goes deep into the gates in your chart specifically from an entrepreneurial perspective, as well as many other aspects of Human Design.

Don't have your report yet and want to get one? Order yours here: spiritualbusinessincubator.com/business-report

The Lines of Your Nodes and Fractal Connections

The lines of your Nodes offer insight into your fractal connections. These lines provide clues about the types of people who are destined to be part of your journey and the themes that define your interactions with them. Understanding the line of your ideal client helps you align your messaging, offers, and approaches to best attract and serve them.

- **Line 1 – The Researchers:** Your ideal clients crave deep knowledge and thorough research. They need clear, well-structured, and foundational information. To attract them, position yourself as an expert with a strong body of knowledge, offering detailed insights and resources that allow them to build confidence in their learning.

- **Line 2 – The Naturals:** These clients are naturally talented but often unaware of their own gifts. They are drawn to ease and flow rather than structure and methodology. To serve them best, offer guidance that is intuitive and fluid, emphasizing experiential learning and allowing them to trust their innate abilities.

- **Line 3 – The Experimenters:** Clients with this line thrive on trial and error. They need an environment where they can test ideas, fail safely, and learn through direct experience. Your approach should encourage adaptability, real-world application, and resilience, providing them with strategies that evolve rather than rigid solutions.

- **Line 4 – The Connectors:** These clients value trust, relationships, and community. They seek connections and thrive in supportive environments. Your role is to create a space where they feel a sense of belonging, whether through group programs, networking opportunities, or strong relational marketing.

- **Line 5 – The Problem-Solvers:** These individuals are visionaries who look for clear, strategic, and effective solutions. They expect leadership and actionable advice. Your messaging should highlight practical outcomes, demonstrating your ability to offer transformative, step-by-step solutions to complex issues.

- **Line 6 – The Role Models:** Clients with this line are drawn to wisdom, mentorship, and long-term transformation. They need to see lived experience and integrity in action. To attract them, establish yourself as an authority who leads by example, sharing both your personal story and the larger perspective of growth and evolution.

Understanding which line is active in your Nodes helps refine how you position yourself in your niche and communicate with your ideal audience. The lines of your Nodes a.k.a. your Fractal Lines offer insight into your fractal connections. These lines provide clues about the types of people who are destined to be part of your journey and the themes that define your interactions with them. By aligning your business with the specific needs of your ideal clients' lines, you can naturally attract those who are most aligned with your unique expertise and energy.

The Quarters of the Incarnation Cross and Niche Alignment

In Human Design, the Quarters of the Incarnation Cross provide insight into the foundational themes that guide an individual's life purpose and influence the type of business they should build. Potential clients will naturally be drawn to entrepreneurs who embody the energy of their respective quarter, as these entrepreneurs serve as guides and facilitators in helping their clients fulfill their own destinies. Here's why an ideal client would be attracted to an entrepreneur whose Incarnation Cross falls within each quarter.

Birthday Between	Incarnation Cross Quarter
February 2 - May 3	Quarter of Initiation
May 4 - August 4	Quarter of Civilization
August 5 - November 5	Quarter of Duality
November 6 - February 1	Quarter of Mutation

- **Quarter of Initiation (Birthdays February 2 - May 3):**
  Entrepreneurs with their Incarnation Cross in this quarter are designed to spark transformation and introduce new paradigms. They thrive in thought leadership, education, and

pioneering unconventional ideas. Clients who seek them out are looking for inspiration, fresh perspectives, and a catalyst for personal or professional growth. These entrepreneurs help their clients break old patterns and step into a new vision of what is possible.

- **Quarter of Civilization (Birthdays May 4 - August 4):**

  These entrepreneurs are builders and creators of structure and lasting impact. Their businesses excel in systems development, organization, and implementing sustainable solutions. Clients who gravitate toward them are often seeking clarity in execution, frameworks for success, and tangible strategies to bring their visions to life. Entrepreneurs in this quarter serve as architects, guiding clients in creating solid foundations for long-term success.

- **Quarter of Duality (Birthdays August 5 - November 5):**

  Entrepreneurs in this quarter excel in relationships, emotional intelligence, and collaboration. Their work often involves coaching, healing, partnerships, and community-building. Clients drawn to them are searching for connection, balance, and guidance in navigating interpersonal dynamics. These entrepreneurs help their clients deepen self-awareness, cultivate meaningful relationships, and create harmony between personal and professional aspects of life.

- **Quarter of Mutation (Birthdays November 6 - February 1):**

  The entrepreneurs in this quarter are disruptors and innovators. They thrive in radical transformation, breakthrough technologies, and revolutionary business models. Clients seeking them are those on the edge of change, eager for a new way of thinking and being. These entrepreneurs help their clients push boundaries, embrace evolution, and step into bold, unconventional paths.

From the perspective of defining your niche, understanding which quarter your Incarnation Cross falls into can help you understand what your most aligned clients are seeking from you more deeply. Design your business in a way that naturally aligns with your energy, making it easier to attract the right clients and opportunities.

Attracting Clients with Energetic Ease

Beyond theoretical knowledge, energetic ease is a powerful indicator of niche alignment. When working with your ideal clients, you should feel a natural flow rather than resistance. If engaging with certain clients feels draining, it may be a sign that you need to refine your niche further.

Practical Application Exercise: Reflection Questions for Niche Clarity

Your niche will evolve as your business grows. It's crucial to have clarity on who you are serving at this moment, as well as who you want to be serving in the future. These can be the same or they can be different, but bringing conscious awareness to this is important. Ask yourself the following questions:

- What are characteristics of my Human Design that influence my aligned niche?
- Are my current clients aligned with that?
- Who am I currently serving and attracting to my business?
- Do I feel energized or drained by my current audience?
- What specific transformation do I offer for my current clients?
- Why do clients seek me out instead of others?
- What shared traits do my best clients have?
- Who do I desire to serve in the future? More of the same? Someone new? A mix?

These reflections help refine your niche and ensure that your business remains in alignment with both your personal fulfillment and market demand.

Common Mistakes to Avoid

Finding the right niche is a delicate balance between clarity and flexibility. Many entrepreneurs struggle with this process, often making mistakes that prevent them from fully stepping into their zone of genius. Here are three common pitfalls to avoid when defining your niche:

- **Trying to Serve Everyone:** One of the biggest mistakes visionary entrepreneurs make is attempting to appeal to a broad audience, believing this will increase their opportunities. However, this often results in watered-down messaging that fails to attract the right clients. Instead of being seen as an authority, you blend in with the crowd, making it harder for your ideal clients to recognize the unique value you offer.

- **Being Too Generic or Too Niche-Specific:** There's a fine line between being too broad and too restrictive. If your niche is too general, your message won't stand out in a crowded market. On the other hand, if it's overly specific, you may feel boxed in, struggling to pivot or evolve as your business grows. The key is to define a niche that is focused enough to establish your authority but flexible enough to allow for organic expansion.

- **Ignoring Alignment with Your Energy and Strengths:** Many entrepreneurs choose their niche based on what they think will be profitable rather than what is truly aligned with their natural energy and strengths. This often leads to frustration, burnout, or difficulty attracting the right clients. By using Human Design to guide your niche, you ensure that your business remains fulfilling, sustainable, and magnetically aligned with your purpose.

A well-defined niche should be a balance between clarity and adaptability. By integrating both strategic business insights and your Human Design, you create a niche that not only attracts the right clients but also supports long-term growth and fulfillment.

CHAPTER 6
CHOOSING YOUR BUSINESS MODEL

In the world of soul-aligned entrepreneurship, your business model is the energetic container that holds your vision, purpose, and the flow of abundance you are creating. It is the operational structure through which your business generates revenue and sustains profitability. But more than that, it is the foundation upon which every decision, about your offers, your team, your energy investment, and your long-term vision, is built.

Far too often, spiritual entrepreneurs dive into creating programs, services, and offers without first establishing the larger structural framework that holds those pieces together. A business model is not your offers; rather, it is the overarching structure that determines how those offers fit together to create a sustainable and scalable path for your success. When chosen with intention, your business model can support your natural gifts, align with your Human Design, and create a flow of ease rather than burnout.

Understanding Business Models in the Real World

To illustrate the difference between a business model and the individual offers within it, let's explore these examples.

- Imagine a community-driven business model where the primary goal is to bring people together and provide value through curated experiences. One version of this could be a local community that offers in-person social events, networking gatherings, and opportunities for members to connect in real life. Another business, also operating under a community-based model, might be an online membership platform that provides virtual networking events, live coaching opportunities, and access to a vault of business templates and resources. Both businesses operate under the same general business model—a service-based, community-driven structure—but the actual services, experiences, and value propositions they offer are entirely different.

- Now, let's take another example: helping entrepreneurs create viral reels on social media. This outcome could be delivered through multiple business models, each requiring a different role from the entrepreneur. One entrepreneur might decide to teach this through a coaching or consulting model, guiding clients step-by-step so they can create their own viral content. Another entrepreneur might build a done-for-you agency model, where a team of experts creates the content on behalf of the client. Both business owners are delivering the same transformation, but the structure of their businesses, the energy they invest, and the way they scale their work are vastly different.

The point of these examples is to show you that similar client needs and wants can be delivered through completely different business models. Since you are the visionary designing this business, make sure your business model is aligned both to your client *and* your unique Human Design.

Why Choosing the Right Business Model Matters

Choosing your business model with clarity and intention is one of the most critical decisions you will make. Without a clearly defined model, it's easy to fall into a cycle of creating random offers that feel disconnected or unsustainable. You might feel pulled in different directions, uncertain whether you should be doing all the work yourself, building a team, or positioning your clients to do the work with your guidance.

Your business model determines all of the following:

- How you invest your time, energy, and resources
- The level of personal involvement you will have in delivering your services
- Whether your business is designed to scale or remain intimate and personalized
- How your offers are structured to fit within a cohesive, profitable ecosystem

But beyond the strategy, your business model should align with your life and business vision. If you desire spaciousness, freedom, and flow, you must choose a model that supports that—not one that locks you into an unsustainable structure. If you thrive in deep one-on-one connections, your model should reflect that, rather than forcing you into high-volume, low-touch offers that drain you.

Aligning Your Role with Your Business Model

Once you establish your business model, here are some key questions to consider.

- What role do you want to play?
- Are you the one doing the work?
- Are you creating a team to fulfill the work?
- Or are your clients doing the work themselves through your guidance and frameworks?

Each of these paths requires different structures, pricing strategies, and energetic investments. When you define this up front, you make more aligned decisions about hiring, scaling, and where to focus your energy for the long term.

The biggest mistake spiritual entrepreneurs make is building businesses that aren't actually designed for the lifestyle and energy flow they desire. Your business model should be a direct reflection of how you want to work, who you want to serve, and how you want abundance to flow into your life. This is the foundation upon which everything else is built.

The Elements of Choosing the Right Business Model for You

At its core, choosing a business model is an act of empowerment. You get to decide how your business is structured, how you serve your clients, and what role you play in delivering your work to the world. This is not a one-size-fits-all decision; it's a deeply personal choice that should align with your vision, your energy, and the way you desire to impact others.

It's important to note that a business model is not just one thing—at least it doesn't have to be, especially considering your Human Design Type. It is also influenced by the ultimate vision for your personal life and business life. You can structure your business to include several models together, just be sure to have the right systems or people to support you in fulfilling your mission.

Key Considerations in Choosing Your Business Model

Your business model is not just about making money; it's about creating an intentional framework that allows you to serve in a way that feels expansive and sustainable. To make the best choice, there are a few key factors to consider.

Who Is Your Client? B2B Versus B2C

Understanding who you are serving will shape how you structure your business. Are you working directly with individual clients, or are you supporting other businesses in their growth?

- **Business-to-Business (B2B):** If you are serving other business owners, your work is positioned to help them generate revenue, streamline operations, or improve their positioning in the marketplace. Your messaging, pricing, and delivery will likely be structured around ROI and business growth.
- **Business-to-Consumer (B2C):** If you are working with individuals for personal transformation—whether through healing, coaching, teaching, or guidance, your business will be built around providing deep personal value. Your marketing will center on emotional connection, transformation, and personal growth.

While some businesses naturally blend both, having clarity on your *primary* audience will help you refine offers, pricing, and messaging in a way that attracts the right people.

Long-Term Vision: How Do You See Your Business Evolving?

Your business model should also align with the long-term vision of how you see yourself and your brand evolving. There are three primary structures to consider.

- **Personal Brand Business:** Your business is centered entirely around *you*, your energy, and your expertise. Clients are drawn to working with you specifically, and your personal presence is deeply integrated into the brand.
- **Business Brand Business:** Your business exists as a separate entity from you. This means you could build a company that operates independently of your personal presence, allowing you to scale, bring on a team, or eventually step back from being the main face.

- **Face of the Business Brand (Hybrid Model):** In this model, you are a recognized figure within your business, but the brand itself is also separate enough that it could eventually grow beyond you. This is a great choice for entrepreneurs who want to be visible in their business but also want the freedom to expand, bring in collaborators, or create something that lasts beyond their personal involvement.

Knowing which path you want to take will impact decisions like naming your business, structuring your offers, and planning for growth.

How Do You Want to Engage with Clients?

Your business model also determines how you interact with your clients and whether your work is primarily in-person, online, or a hybrid of both. Each has its own energetic demands and logistical considerations.

- **Fully In-Person:** If you thrive in direct, face-to-face interactions, you may want to build a business that revolves around live events, retreats, or in-person coaching and healing sessions. This model works well for those who love the energy of physical connection but it requires a location-based strategy.
- **Fully Online:** If you desire freedom and flexibility, an online-based business model allows you to serve clients worldwide without geographic limitations. This can include digital courses, memberships, virtual coaching, and online group programs.
- **Hybrid (A Blend of Both):** Some entrepreneurs prefer a mix, offering online resources alongside in-person experiences. For example, you might provide virtual coaching sessions but host annual live retreats. Or you may build an online membership with occasional in-person networking events.

The key is to choose a model that aligns with your natural strengths, lifestyle desires, and how you best connect with your clients.

How Will You Deliver?

Beyond just knowing who you serve and how you interact with them, it's also important to determine how you want to deliver the actual transformation your business provides. There are three overarching categories of service delivery:

- **Done-For-You (DFY):** In this model, your business does the work on behalf of the client. This is common in service-based businesses such as branding agencies, social media management, or copywriting services. The entrepreneur (or their team) completes the work while the client benefits from the outcome.

- **Done-With-You (DWY):** Here, the work is a collaborative effort. The client is actively involved in the process, often through coaching, consulting, or guided implementation. This model is ideal for those who enjoy teaching, mentoring, and providing hands-on guidance.

- **Do-It-Yourself (DIY):** This model provides clients with the knowledge, tools, or resources they need to achieve results independently. It often includes courses, memberships, books, and self-paced programs. This is a great choice for those who want to scale their impact while minimizing one-on-one client time.

Many businesses use a combination of these models. For instance, you might offer a DFY high-ticket service while also providing a DIY course for those who want a more accessible option. The key is choosing what aligns with your natural strengths and the way you want to work.

Your Business Model Is Your Structural and Energetic Foundation

Your business model is not just a strategic decision; it's an energetic one. It determines how you will show up, how you will scale, and whether your work feels aligned or draining.

Many spiritual entrepreneurs get caught in the trap of choosing a model that doesn't actually match their energy, leading to burnout and misalignment. Instead, approach this decision with intention. Does your model give you the freedom you desire? Does it allow you to serve in a way that feels expansive? Does it align with your long-term vision?

By consciously selecting a business model that honors your energy, supports your vision, and aligns with your strengths, you are setting yourself up for sustainable, soul-aligned success.

Aligning Your Business Model with Human Design

Your business model acts as the structure that holds and moves energy, determining how your business functions, how you serve your clients, and how abundance flows through your work. When approached through the lens of Human Design, your business model becomes an intentional framework that supports your energy as the visionary, the energy of your clients, and the energy required to keep your business running smoothly. When you align your business model with your Human Design, you create a business that feels expansive rather than restrictive, natural rather than forced, and deeply fulfilling rather than energetically draining. To do this, we must consider key aspects of your Human Design chart to ensure your business model is designed to work with your energy rather than against it.

Human Design Elements to Consider When Choosing Your Business Model

Energy Type: How Your Aura Interacts with Others

Your Human Design Type is one of the most important considerations in determining your business model. Your Energy Type dictates how your personal energy flows and how your aura interacts with others, whether that's clients, team members, or your audience.

Each Type has different needs when it comes to structuring their business, especially regarding how much interaction they desire, how they best make decisions, and what business model will feel the most sustainable.

Manifestors: Creating in Bursts and Maintaining Freedom

Manifestors are here to initiate and bring new ideas into the world. They thrive in business models that allow them to work in creative bursts rather than requiring consistent, day-to-day interactions with clients.

- **Business Model Considerations:** Manifestors may do well with self-led digital courses, licensing models, or high-level consulting where they set things in motion but don't need to maintain ongoing interaction.
- **Potential Challenges:** A business model that requires constant availability (e.g., daily coaching or client work) may lead to burnout unless they have strong boundaries.

Generators: Sustainable, Consistent Energy

Generators have access to sustainable energy, and they thrive when doing work they genuinely love. Their business model should allow them to focus on deep work and responding to what excites them.

- **Business Model Considerations:** Generators can thrive in coaching, teaching, or service-based businesses where they are doing hands-on work they feel deeply connected to.
- **Potential Challenges:** If they build a model around work they don't enjoy, they will experience frustration and exhaustion, even if the business is profitable.

Manifesting Generators: Multi-Passionate and Fast-Paced

Manifesting Generators (MG) are *multi-dimensional creators* who thrive on variety, efficiency, and speed. They need a business model that allows them to pivot, innovate, and streamline.

- **Business Model Considerations:** MGs may do well with a hybrid model, such as a mix of digital products, coaching, and hands-on services. They also thrive in automated models that give them the freedom to move between passions without being tied to one offer.
- **Potential Challenges:** If they try to limit themselves to a rigid structure, they may feel trapped and lose momentum.

Projectors: Business Models That Honor Rest and Insight

Projectors are here to guide others and see them deeply, not to work long hours in traditional business models. They need a business model that prioritizes value over volume, where they are compensated well for their insights rather than their time.

- **Business Model Considerations:** Projectors do well with high-ticket consulting, personalized mentorship, or leveraged offers (e.g., group programs or prerecorded teachings).
- **Potential Challenges:** A business model that requires nonstop client work without proper rest will quickly lead to burnout.

Reflectors: Fluid, Community-Oriented Business Models

Reflectors are deeply in tune with the energy around them and thrive in business models that allow them to observe, assess, and share their wisdom. They often do best in community-driven businesses or roles where they can reflect trends back to others.

- **Business Model Considerations:** Facilitation-based models (such as curating communities, leading group experiences, or providing intuitive guidance) are ideal.
- **Potential Challenges:** A business model that is too rigid or high-pressure can feel overwhelming and stifling.

Profile: The Role You Play in Your Business

Your Human Design Profile represents the role you naturally embody in your business and how people see you. When choosing a business model, it's essential to align with what your audience naturally seeks from you (Personality Line) while also honoring what you need for yourself (Design Line).

- **Personality Line (first number in your Profile):** What people are drawn to you for.
- **Design Line (second number in your Profile):** What you need to feel supported and aligned.

Each Profile Line offers insight into the best business model fit:

- **Line 1 (Investigator):** Needs research, depth, and solid foundations. Prefers structured teaching models or expertise-driven businesses.
- **Line 2 (Natural):** Thrives in ease and flow. Often does best when business is built around personal mastery rather than forcing structured strategies.
- **Line 3 (Experimenter):** Learns through trial and error. Needs freedom to test, tweak, and iterate business models rather than rigid plans.
- **Line 4 (Networker):** Community-driven. Thrives in models that involve deep relationship-building and connection.
- **Line 5 (Problem-Solver):** Seen as a guide and leader. Works well with high-level coaching, consulting, and broad impact strategies.
- **Line 6 (Role Model):** Moves through three phases in business (learning, experimenting, and mastery). Often thrives in a long-term mentorship model.

For example, if you are someone with a Line 4 (Networker) in your Profile, you may naturally build relationships and community. A community-based business model might be an organic fit. However, if you don't have strong Line 4 energy, forcing yourself to build a community-driven business because "it's what everyone does" could lead to exhaustion and resistance.

Human Design Environments: The Energetic Vibe of Your Business Model

In Human Design, your Environment represents the physical and energetic space where you are most aligned, supported, and therefore, where you thrive. It influences how you process information, interact with others, and structure your business. When your business model aligns with your Environment, you naturally feel more energized, clear, and successful because your business is set up in a way that supports how you best operate and engage with the world. Each Environment brings its own unique energy, influencing how you design your offers, structure client interactions, and build your business ecosystem. Let's explore how different models align with each of the six Human Design Environments.

Markets: The Business Model of Exchange and Variety

Energetic Vibe: Dynamic, ever-changing, fluid exchange of energy, ideas, and resources.

Aligned Business Models: Marketplace-based businesses, coaching collectives, product-based businesses, networking-driven models.

If you have a **Markets Environment**, you thrive in spaces of exchange, variety, and movement. Your ideal business model will allow you to offer, trade, and sell in a way that feels fluid and evolving rather than fixed or rigid. You may naturally enjoy trying new offers, experimenting with different price points, and engaging with multiple streams of income.

Aligned Business Models for Markets Environments

- **Membership or Subscription Models:** A membership-based business provides an ongoing exchange of value, where members gain access to exclusive content, coaching, or services in exchange for a recurring fee. This model thrives on community engagement and dynamic offerings that evolve over time.

- **Marketplace-Based Business:** A digital or physical marketplace allows for buying, selling, and exchanging products or services, such as running an online store, a platform for healers and coaches to list their services, or a knowledge-sharing hub.

- **Service-Based with Customizable Offers:** Having a menu of offerings, such as custom coaching packages, personalized services, or flexible pricing tiers, allows you to adapt based on demand and keep things fresh.

- **Frequent Launch-Based Business Model:** Instead of running an evergreen offer, a frequent-launch style allows you to generate excitement, test new offers, and continuously attract new clients. This could include live workshops, short-term programs, or seasonal product drops.

Considerations

If you try to box yourself into one fixed offer for too long, you may feel stagnant. Allow room for pivoting, refreshing, and testing new business directions.

Caves: The Business Model of Privacy and Selectivity

Energetic Vibe: Protection, exclusivity, deep one-on-one or small-group interactions.

Aligned Business Models: High-ticket services, small-group coaching, VIP experiences, and boutique businesses.

A **Caves Environment** is all about safety, intimacy, and control over access. You thrive in business models that allow you to choose who you work with, create exclusive offerings, and cultivate deep trust with clients.

Aligned Business Models for Caves Environments

- **High-Ticket, Selective Coaching or Consulting:** Instead of working with large groups, you may prefer a one-on-one or small-group model where you deeply customize your work for each client.
- **VIP Days and Private Intensives:** This model allows clients to work with you in an exclusive, high-impact way over a short period, providing deep transformation without requiring ongoing commitments.
- **Private Memberships or Invite-Only Programs:** A closed-circle business model works well, where only select members can join. This could be an application-based coaching program, an exclusive mastermind, or a private healing circle.
- **Done-For-You Boutique Services:** If you offer a service (e.g., branding, copywriting, business strategy), you might prefer working with a small number of high-caliber clients in an intimate, confidential setting.

Considerations

Avoid business models that require constant public exposure, high-volume client work, or large-scale group interactions. You will thrive when you control the access points to your business and maintain a sense of energetic protection.

Shores: The Business Model of Balance and Perspective

Energetic Vibe: Bridging two worlds, seeing both sides, bringing contrast together.

Aligned Business Models: Hybrid business models, teaching and coaching, and transformation-focused businesses.

A **Shores Environment** thrives in contrast and perspective. You likely see multiple angles to a problem and enjoy bringing two different worlds together (e.g., spirituality and business, healing and strategy, creativity and structure). Your business model should reflect this bridge-building energy.

Aligned Business Models for Shores Environments

- **Hybrid Business Models:** A mix of digital offerings and in-person experiences allows you to balance structure and connection (e.g., a coaching program with virtual modules but in-person retreats).
- **Transformation Coaching or Mentorship:** Shores people often thrive as guides for transformation, helping clients navigate major life or business shifts. Your model might be focused on personal development, business coaching, or intuitive guidance.
- **Online Courses with Live Components:** A structured online program with live coaching calls or Q&A sessions allows you to offer a blend of structured learning and real-time interaction.
- **Dual-Focus Business Models:** Your business might combine two seemingly opposite worlds (e.g., spirituality and

business, healing and technology, or science and intuition) and create unique offers from this intersection.

Considerations

Avoid business models that are too one-sided, for example, being fully in-person with no digital presence or fully automated with no human connection. You will thrive in a model that allows you to exist in both worlds and shift between them as needed.

Kitchens: The Business Model of Innovation and Creation

Energetic Vibe: Experimentation, alchemy, behind-the-scenes creation.

Aligned Business Models: Course creation, content-heavy business models, and product development.

If you have a **Kitchens Environment**, you are here to experiment, innovate, and create something new. Your business model should give you space to develop ideas behind the scenes, refine them, and bring them to life in a way that benefits others.

Aligned Business Models for Kitchens Environments

- **Course and Program Development:** You may thrive in a model where you create structured courses, self-paced programs, or signature methodologies that others can learn from.
- **Product-Based Businesses:** Whether physical or digital, creating tools, guides, or transformational products (e.g., journals, tarot decks, Human Design resources) may feel deeply aligned.
- **Intellectual Property and Licensing:** Kitchens people often develop unique frameworks that they may want to have licensed or taught by others, allowing them to work behind the scenes while still impacting others.
- **Behind-the-Scenes Business Models:** You may do best in support roles, content creation, or consulting that allows you to stay out of the spotlight while still shaping the industry.

Considerations

If you try to force yourself into high-client interaction roles or a business model that requires constant visibility, you may feel depleted. Focus on building sustainable assets behind the scenes that allow your creations to shine.

Valleys: The Business Model of Community and Depth

Energetic Vibe: Deep connection, community engagement, niche mastery.

Aligned Business Models: Community-based models, niche expertise, coaching containers with long-term depth.

A **Valleys Environment** thrives on building deep relationships and serving a niche community over time. Your business model should allow you to connect with people, build strong networks, and become a trusted authority in your space.

Aligned Business Models for Valleys Environments

- **Retreat and Event-Based Models:** Immersive, in-person or virtual retreats align beautifully with the Valleys Environment. Retreats provide an enclosed, intimate setting where participants can engage deeply, reflect, and connect with others over a longer period.
- **Specialized Niche Businesses:** Valleys people thrive when they become experts in a particular area, attracting long-term clients who seek their specific knowledge and wisdom.
- **Long-Term Coaching, Membership, or Advisory Programs:** Long-term coaching programs that span six to twelve months (or longer) allow you to develop deep, transformational relationships with your clients.

Considerations

Avoid broad, generalized business models. You will feel most aligned when your business model allows you to nurture relationships and go deep into one area of expertise.

Mountains: The Business Model of Vision and Elevation

Energetic Vibe: Big-picture thinking, observation, strategic leadership.

Aligned Business Models: High-level consulting, thought leadership, vision-driven businesses.

A **Mountains Environment** thrives on perspective, strategy, and high-level vision. Your business model should allow you to guide, teach, and lead from an elevated space, rather than being in the day-to-day details.

Aligned Business Models for Mountains Environments

- **High-Level Consulting and Advisory Roles:** Instead of working one-on-one with clients in an execution-based role, Mountains entrepreneurs often excel in high-level strategy, advising businesses, or providing mentorship at scale.
- **Speaking and Thought Leadership:** Mountains people thrive in roles where they share their wisdom on a larger scale, influencing and educating many people at once rather than working with individuals.
- **Automated Business Models:** Instead of relying only on direct client work, a Mountains entrepreneur might develop and sell products, courses, or frameworks that allow others to benefit from their knowledge without needing direct access to them.

Considerations

Avoid business models that require too much hands-on execution. Your strength lies in big-picture strategy and leadership.

Practical Application Exercise: Aligning Your Business Model with Your Human Design

To integrate these insights, take a moment to reflect and ask yourself:

- What business model allows me to serve in alignment with my Human Design?
- How do my Type, Profile, and Environment shape the way I want to interact with clients?
- What business structure allows me to sustain my energy long-term?

Now look at the business model or structure you currently have in place. Is it the right one to fulfill your business mission with the most ease? Is it the right one for the role you desire to play in your business? If yes, keep moving forward. If no, consider evolving your business to a new model.

Common Mistakes to Avoid

- **Following the Hype Instead of Your Energy:** Just because a business model is trendy (e.g., "Everyone should build a membership community!") doesn't mean it's aligned for you. Your design—not external trends—dictates your flow.
- **Forcing a Business Model That Doesn't Match Your Energy:** If your model requires constant energy output, social engagement, or structured consistency that doesn't fit your design, you will feel resistance and burnout.
- **Ignoring How You Best Make Decisions:** Your Authority (Sacral, Emotional, Splenic, etc.) plays a role in how you should decide on a business model. Trust your decision-making Strategy instead of rushing into choices based on external pressure.

CHAPTER 7

DEFINING YOUR SERVICES AND OFFERS

What's the Difference Between Services and Offers?

In the entrepreneurial space, I've noticed that many business owners experience a great deal of confusion between services and offers. While these terms are often used interchangeably, they are distinct components of a business model. Understanding their differences will help you structure your business in a way that feels aligned and clear, both for yourself and for the clients you serve.

Deeper Dive into Services and Choosing Yours

Your **services** are the tangible deliverables you provide to your clients to help them achieve their desired outcome. This is what you *do* in your business—the actual work you perform that leads to transformation. Services encompass the direct actions, methods, and tools you use to support clients.

Think of services as the core elements of your business. They might include one-on-one coaching, group mentorship, content creation, digital courses, healing sessions, consulting, or any other practical way you deliver results to your clients. Services are what create the impact your clients experience and are the fundamental building blocks of your business.

Understanding How to Create Compelling Offers

Your **offer**, on the other hand, is the packaging of your services into a structured experience that facilitates transformation. The word *offer* is commonly used in business discussions, but many entrepreneurs don't realize that an offer is more than just selling a single service. An offer is a curated combination of services, resources, and incentives positioned in a way that directly aligns with your ideal client's needs and desires.

An offer isn't just about what you do, it's about how you present and deliver it in a way that makes sense for your business and the transformation your clients seek. It involves the structure, timeline, pricing, bonuses, and any additional elements that enhance the client's experience.

For example, an emotional abuse recovery coach might provide services such as private coaching, a virtual support community, guided meditations, and self-paced courses. They could then craft different offers by packaging these services in various ways. One offer might be a membership community where members receive access to courses and a group forum, while another offer could include one-on-one coaching calls for those seeking more personalized guidance. To incentivize sign-ups, they might add a bonus, such as a free coaching session for those who join within a limited timeframe or create urgency by announcing an upcoming price increase. These strategies don't change the services provided, but they shape how those services are packaged, positioned, and sold.

Why This Matters

There Are Countless Ways to Structure Your Business

One of the most liberating truths in business is that there is no single, right way to build your offers. You have the freedom to create a business model that aligns with your unique strengths, Human Design, and the needs of your ideal clients. There are more possibilities than I can cover in this book: What's most important is that you build a structure that feels both exciting to sell and sustainable to deliver.

Your Services Are the Core of Your Client's Transformation

The services you provide are what facilitate the transformation your clients experience. They are the tangible methods through which you deliver results. Whether you offer coaching, healing, education, or a combination of modalities, the services are what create the outcomes that make a difference in your client's life and business.

You Want to Be Excited About Selling and Delivering Your Offers

Many spiritual entrepreneurs struggle with selling because they don't feel fully aligned with the way their offers are structured. If you create an offer purely based on what you think will sell—but it doesn't feel right to you—you'll subconsciously resist promoting it. Your energy around your offer matters. It's essential to design offers that you feel *excited* to sell and deliver so you can show up confidently and enthusiastically when presenting them to your audience.

Your Services and Offers Should Be Designed with Intention

Every service and offer you create should be designed with a specific component of your niche in mind, while still aligning with your overall business mission. Your offers should be crafted to serve different levels of client needs, ensuring that they seamlessly integrate into the bigger picture of your business. This intentional approach allows you to build a business ecosystem where each offer serves a distinct purpose, making it easier for clients to find the right fit for their decision to work with you. Clarity around your services and offers will help you build a sustainable, aligned, and thriving business. By designing offers that excite you and strategically align with your clients' needs, you'll create a business that not only supports your mission but also provides a seamless, intuitive experience for those you are meant to serve.

Business Elements: Structuring Your Services for Maximum Impact

Understanding the different types of services you can provide allows you to build a business that feels aligned with your skills, expertise, and the transformation you offer your clients. Below is a breakdown of various service types and how they function within your business.

Services as Deliverables

Each service you offer is a method of delivering transformation to your clients. Here's how different service types function:

- **Consultations:** These are advisory sessions where you tell clients what they should do based on your expertise. Ideal for strategists, consultants, and advisors.
- **Coaching:** Unlike consulting, coaching helps clients uncover their own path through guided self-discovery and support.
- **Experiential Sessions:** One-on-one service-based interactions where a client receives direct support during a scheduled timeframe (e.g., healing and salon appointments, etc.).
- **Webinars:** Short-term teaching or training sessions to share your knowledge.
- **Workshops:** Interactive and process-oriented learning experiences that guide participants through transformation.
- **Programs:** Structured, often live, step-by-step experiences designed to help participants achieve a particular outcome.
- **Courses:** Prerecorded or live educational content delivered in a structured format.
- **Retreats:** Immersive, experience-based events over multiple days.
- **Events:** This includes conferences, networking events, and in-person gatherings of varying scales.
- **VIP Intensives:** High-touch, short-term sessions designed to achieve rapid results.
- **Resources:** Digital products like templates, checklists, and audio guides.

- **Your Unique Service:** You have the freedom to create whatever feels most aligned with your vision!

Components of an Offer: Crafting with Intention

An offer is more than just a collection of services, it's a strategically designed package that communicates value, creates desire, and provides a clear path to transformation. Whether you're building a high-ticket coaching program, a digital course, or a done-for-you service, the way you structure your offer directly impacts how your clients perceive it and, ultimately, whether they buy. Through both traditional business frameworks and modern online business coaching programs, six key components consistently emerge as essential in crafting an irresistible offer.

1. **The Core Program: Defining What You Are Delivering**

   Every offer is centered around a core service, product, or program, also known as the primary thing you are delivering. This could be any or all of the following:

   - A coaching program that provides a step-by-step transformation
   - A course or workshop designed to teach specific skills
   - A membership or group experience for ongoing support
   - A done-for-you service where you complete work on behalf of the client
   - And so many more. Literally any way you want to serve people!

   Clarity is key; what exactly is your client signing up for? A well-structured core program makes it easy for potential buyers to understand what they are getting and how it benefits them.

2. **The Promise: The Transformation or Result Clients Will Receive**

   Every successful offer is built around a clear transformation or outcome. Clients don't just buy services, they also invest in results. Your promise should answer these specific questions:

- What will your clients achieve after working with you?
- How will their life or business change?
- Why does this matter to them?

A strong promise is both specific and compelling. It should communicate the tangible or emotional shift your clients will experience. Instead of saying, "This program helps you grow your business," a stronger promise would be: "By the end of this program, you will have a fully booked client calendar and a streamlined strategy that attracts high-quality leads consistently."

3. **Pricing Considerations: Positioning Your Offer for the Right Audience**

Pricing is more than just a number; it's a strategic decision that impacts how your offer is perceived. There are multiple factors to consider:

- Free Versus Paid: Is this a lead-generation offer to attract potential clients, or is it a revenue-generating service?
- Primary Purpose: Is your offer designed to introduce people to your work, provide deep transformation, or scale your business?
- Buyer Psychology: Are you targeting emotional buyers (who invest based on feeling and transformation) or analytical buyers (who focus on logic and details)?
- Time Investment Versus Value Provided: Does the price reflect the depth of transformation, not just the time spent delivering it?
- Market Positioning: Are you positioning your offer as a luxury, mid-tier, or cost-effective service? Each pricing tier attracts a different type of buyer.
- Client Expectations: Are your clients looking for a quick win, a high-touch experience, or an immersive, premium-level transformation?

Your pricing should align with both the value you provide and the expectations of your ideal client.

4. Urgency and Scarcity: Encouraging Commitment

People often delay decisions, even when they want something. Creating urgency and scarcity helps potential buyers take action sooner rather than later.

- Time-Based Incentives: Enrollment deadlines, limited-time bonuses, or upcoming price increases motivate clients to act.
- Limited Availability: Restricting the number of spots in a program or setting a cap on availability increases perceived value. (Example: "Only ten spots available for personalized coaching.")
- Exclusive Access: Creating VIP experiences or early-bird pricing for action-takers builds excitement and urgency.

When implemented authentically, urgency and scarcity make it easier for clients to make a confident decision.

5. Bonuses: Enhancing the Perceived Value

Bonuses are extra add-ons that make your offer feel even more valuable. A well-designed bonus should complement your core offer and address potential objections.

- If your program requires a learning curve, include a quick-start guide to help clients get results faster.
- If potential clients worry about staying accountable, offer bonus live Q&A calls or coaching check-ins.
- If they need additional tools, provide exclusive templates, workbooks, or resources.

Bonuses should feel like added benefit, not unnecessary fluff. Well-crafted bonuses help justify the price and increase conversions. (Note, in business, *conversion* is the process of a person moving through your marketing process or client journey.) This could be by getting their contact information or formally becoming a paid client. Thus, the more conversions you have the more evidence you have that the item you are offering is valued by your target market.

6. **Guarantees: Reducing Risk and Increasing Trust**

A guarantee removes fear and hesitation by offering clients reassurance. Different types of guarantees help build trust and confidence in your offer.

- Money-Back Guarantee: A traditional risk-reversal technique. (Example: "If you don't see results in thirty days, get a full refund.")
- Time Extension Guarantee: Offers additional support if results aren't achieved in the expected timeframe. (Example: "Stay in the program an extra month for free if you haven't made your first sale.")
- Satisfaction Assurance: A commitment to making sure clients feel supported. (Example: "If you're not 100 percent happy, we'll work with you until you are.")

Guarantees remove perceived risk, making it easier for potential clients to commit to your offer.

A well-structured offer isn't just about what you're selling, it's about how you package, position, and present it to align with your ideal clients. By thoughtfully designing each component, you create an offer that is not only valuable but also compelling, sustainable, and perfectly suited to your unique energy and expertise.

Human Design Elements That Influence Service and Offer Creation

Your Human Design significantly influences how you create, structure, and sell your offers. Choosing which services your business delivers is an involved process. By incorporating these core elements of your Human Design, you can ensure that your business aligns with your natural strengths, making it easier to sustain long-term success and satisfaction. Here's a list of the Human Design aspects I recommend using when considering what services would be best aligned for you and the clients you are meant to serve.

- **Type:** Your Human Design Type determines your energy dynamics, productivity patterns, and natural workflow.
- **Profile Lines:** Your Profile impacts your working style, engagement with clients, and how you best structure your business.
- **Gates:** These reflect your natural gifts and areas of expertise. Identifying your strongest gates can help refine the transformation you offer and how you communicate it to your audience.
- **Channels:** Defined channels represent strong, consistent gifts. These can serve as indicators of the kind of services you'll excel at providing.
- **Centers:** Understanding your centers helps determine how you show up in your business.
- **Environment:** This determines the setting where you and your clients feel most at ease. It's crucial when designing your business structure. Aligning your Environment to your service model increases sustainability and ease in your business.
- **Strategy and Authority:** This is how you best make decisions, which directly affects your business structure, pricing strategies, and sales approach.

By integrating Human Design into the creation of your service structure and offer, you build a business that works with your natural strengths rather than against them, allowing for alignment, ease, and longevity. Your services are the way you fulfill your business mission, so make sure you are being intentional with how you set up this important aspect of your business.

The way I teach entrepreneurs to use these aspects of their Human Design in mapping out their services looks at all of these components separately, then also together as a whole. This is part of the nuanced, service design process we offer inside my courses and programs. However, by knowing these Human Design aspects are the ones that influence your services, then you can start to explore them on your own as well! Even better, you can get your personalized Entrepreneur by Design report, which is essentially a custom fifty-plus-page book explaining most Human Design aspects specifically through the lens of entrepreneurship. If you are looking for more hands-on support with this, go to spiritualbusinessincubator.com to explore future business planning cohorts and more.

Practical Application Exercise: Reflect on Your Services

Reflection is a crucial step in ensuring your business is aligned with your energy and mission. Use the following questions to deepen your understanding of how your services and offers support both your clients and you.

1. **What is the client experience you are delivering?**
    - How do clients feel when they engage with your services or offers?
    - Is the path smooth and intuitive, or does it need refinement?
    - What emotions and transformations do you want clients to experience?

2. **How does your Human Design influence your offer structure?**
    - Are you creating offers that align with your natural workflow and strengths?
    - Are you leveraging your defined centers for consistency and your undefined centers for insight and wisdom?
    - Do your offers allow you to work in a way that feels sustainable and enjoyable?

3. **Are you designing services that excite you and align with your energy?**
    - Do you feel drained or energized by your current offerings?
    - Would shifting your delivery method (live versus prerecorded, one-on-one versus group) make your work feel more aligned?

- Is there anything you feel called to add or remove from your service suite?

4. **How does your pricing and positioning reflect your business values?**

   - Is your pricing based on the true value of transformation, or are you undercharging due to fear?
   - Does your pricing strategy align with your business goals and ideal clients?
   - How does positioning your offer influence the perception of your brand?

5. **Are you creating an intuitive pathway for client growth?**

   - Do your offers provide a clear process from entry-level engagement to deeper transformation?
   - How do your services and offers interconnect to support long-term client relationships?
   - Are there gaps in your current offer suite that could be filled to better serve your audience?

Taking time to reflect on these aspects will not only refine your offerings but also help ensure your business is both fulfilling and successful. Adjustments made from a place of alignment and self-awareness will lead to a business that is both impactful and sustainable.

Common Mistakes to Avoid

The process of creating and selling offers must continue to evolve, but there are common mistakes that entrepreneurs make which can lead to stagnation. Awareness of these pitfalls can help you refine your approach and create a more aligned and profitable business.

1. **Constantly changing your core deliverables due to lack of results:** Many entrepreneurs assume that if an offer isn't selling, the service itself must be wrong. However, more often than not, the issue lies in marketing, messaging, or positioning rather than the deliverable itself. Instead of scrapping an entire service or offer, assess whether your messaging is clear, if you

are reaching the right audience, and if you have effectively communicated the transformation your offer provides. It is often easier to tweak your offer structure, pricing, or marketing strategy than to completely overhaul what you offer.

2. **Randomly creating services or offers without market research:** Just because an idea excites you doesn't mean it will automatically resonate with your audience. Before developing a new service or offer, conduct market research, engage with your existing community, and validate demand. This could include polling your audience, having direct conversations with ideal clients, and analyzing competitors. Ensure that what you create meets a specific need or desire within your target market rather than simply something you assume they want.

3. **Focusing only on the short term and not considering the bigger business vision:** It's easy to get caught up in launching something quickly to generate immediate revenue, but every service and offer should fit into your long-term business strategy. Instead of building disconnected offers, ensure your services flow logically and nurture clients through a journey, leading them to deeper engagement over time.

4. **Lack of intentional pricing and positioning strategy:** Many entrepreneurs undercharge out of fear or overprice without considering value perception. Your pricing should align with the transformation you provide, the type of clients you want to attract, and the level of service involved. Consider the following:

   • Is your price positioning you as a luxury, mid-tier, or cost-effective offer?
   • Are you clearly communicating the value and results of your offer?
   • Does your pricing match your effort, time investment, and expertise?

By recognizing and avoiding these common mistakes, you can refine your business approach, build offers that feel aligned, and create a sustainable model that supports both you and your clients.

CHAPTER **8**

INTENTIONALLY CHOOSING ALIGNED MARKETING PATHWAYS

What Is Marketing, Anyway?

Marketing is often misunderstood as merely promoting a product or service, but it is so much more than that. At its core, marketing is the strategic process of communicating about and promoting offerings in a way that resonates with the right people. It involves reaching potential clients, building relationships, and creating value to naturally guide them toward making a buying decision. When marketing is done in alignment with your business goals, audience needs, and preferred methods of engagement, it becomes a seamless process that feels natural rather than forced.

One of the most crucial aspects of marketing is ensuring that it aligns with your unique energy and business model. Traditional marketing methods may not feel right for everyone, which is why it is essential to design a marketing strategy that works for you and attracts your ideal clients in a way that feels organic and aligned.

Taking People Through the Know, Like, and Trust Process

One of the foundational principles of effective marketing is the *Know, Like, and Trust* process. People cannot work with you if they do not know you exist, like you/your business, and trust that you will deliver the solution or outcome they desire. This process represents the pathway a potential client takes from discovering you for the first time to feeling confident enough to invest in what you offer. Here's an overview of what happens in each of these phases.

Know: The Awareness Phase – Getting on Their Radar

Before someone can engage with your business, they first need to know you exist. This is the visibility stage, where your primary goal is to increase awareness and make your brand discoverable. If your ideal audience doesn't know about you, they can't become a client.

Key Strategies to Increase Visibility

- **Content Marketing:** Sharing valuable, educational, or inspiring content through blogs, podcasts, social media, or YouTube.
- **SEO (Search Engine Optimization) and Searchability:** Optimizing your website, content, and profiles so that people searching for solutions can find you.
- **Collaborations and Partnerships:** Tapping into aligned audiences through guest podcasting, joint ventures, or social media takeovers.
- **Paid Advertising:** Using targeted ads to get in front of your ideal audience faster.

The Goal: To get your name and message in front of the right people so they become aware of what you do.

Like: The Resonance Phase – Creating a Genuine Connection

Once someone knows about you, the next step is for them to feel a connection to your brand, personality, and values. People buy from those they resonate with; they want to feel that your energy, perspective, and way of doing things align with them.

Ways to Build Likability and Connection

- **Authenticity:** Show up as *you*. Let your personality shine through in your content, storytelling, and interactions.
- **Brand Messaging:** Make sure your brand voice reflects your values, mission, and unique approach.
- **Engagement and Community Building:** Respond to comments, engage in conversations, and make people feel seen.
- **Behind-the-Scenes Content:** Share your insights and personal experiences to create a more personal connection.

The Goal: To create an emotional connection so people not only understand what you do but also feel aligned with your energy and message.

Trust: The Confidence Phase – Demonstrating Credibility and Value

Even if someone knows and likes you, they won't invest until they trust that you can actually deliver results. Trust is built through consistency, credibility, and value. People need to feel confident that your expertise, approach, and offer will genuinely help them.

Ways to Build Trust and Authority

- **Providing Value Consistently:** Share actionable insights, case studies, and free resources that demonstrate your knowledge.
- **Client Testimonials and Success Stories:** Social proof builds confidence and highlights how you've helped others succeed.
- **Clear and Transparent Messaging:** Be up front about who your offer is for, what it includes, and what outcomes to expect.
- **Consistency in Branding and Presence:** A cohesive, professional brand builds subconscious trust. Show up consistently rather than sporadically.

The Goal: To create a sense of certainty, potential clients should feel safe, confident, and excited about investing in your offer.

To successfully guide people through this process, you must intentionally map out how each marketing activity supports movement from one stage to the next. Many entrepreneurs market haphazardly, hoping that showing up online or sharing a post will be enough. Instead, it's important to create a structured marketing pathway that strategically nurtures your audience and provides clear next steps at each phase of the client journey.

Helping People Understand What You Have to Offer

Marketing should never feel like pushing or convincing. That is a sure-fire way to lose aligned clients. It should be about clearly communicating the transformation and value to your offers so that potential clients can make an informed decision. The goal is to empower people with the information they need to determine if what you provide is the right fit for them.

Aligned marketing does the following:

- Creates clarity around how your offers solve specific problems or fulfill desires
- Provides education about your approach, process, and philosophy
- Helps potential clients self-identify whether they resonate with you and the transformation you facilitate

When done correctly, marketing is not about forcing people into a sale but about allowing them to naturally move toward a decision because they genuinely see the value and alignment in what you offer.

Why Intentional Marketing Matters

Many entrepreneurs struggle with marketing because they lack a clear strategy. Without intentionality, marketing can feel overwhelming, ineffective, or inconsistent. By defining where and how you engage with potential clients and ensuring each marketing effort has a clear purpose, you create a streamlined, sustainable, and effective marketing pathway.

Defining Where and What You Are Communicating

Marketing is most effective when it is intentional. Instead of spreading yourself thin across multiple platforms with no clear strategy, focus on defining *where* you engage with potential clients and *what* you are communicating at each stage. Every marketing effort should serve a specific purpose in moving people closer to working with you.

Ask yourself:

- Where are my ideal clients already spending time? (Social media, podcasts, live events, email lists, etc.)
- What do they need to hear from me to move forward?
- How can I make each interaction meaningful and valuable?

By being clear about where you show up and what you communicate, you create a focused and strategic marketing pathway that naturally leads to conversion.

Business Elements for Choosing Your Marketing Pathways

Designing an effective marketing strategy requires understanding how people move through the client journey and structuring your approach to meet them at every stage. Rather than relying on random marketing tactics, intentional marketing aligns each activity with a specific purpose and stage, ensuring that your messaging and outreach lead to actual conversions.

The Four Core Marketing Activities: A Strategic Approach to Consistent Growth

At any given moment, your marketing efforts should be intentional and strategic, designed to support one of four key objectives. Many entrepreneurs struggle with marketing because they approach it in a scattered way: posting content without a clear purpose, focusing too much on one area while neglecting others, or expecting immediate sales without building trust first. When you structure your marketing around these four core activities, you create a balanced system that consistently attracts, nurtures, and converts aligned clients. Let's dive deeper into the core marketing activities that need to occur.

Stage 1: Create Awareness and Visibility – Helping New People Discover You

Before someone can engage with your business, they first need to know you exist. The goal of this phase is to increase your reach and put your message in front of the right audience so that new people are consistently entering your world.

Effective Strategies for Increasing Awareness

- **Social Media and Content Marketing:** Posting valuable content on platforms where your ideal clients spend time.
- **SEO and Searchable Content:** Creating blogs, YouTube videos, and Pinterest pins that make you discoverable.
- **Guest Features and Collaborations:** Expanding your audience by appearing on podcasts, summits, or partnering with aligned businesses.
- **Paid Advertising:** Running targeted ads to amplify your reach.

The Goal: Expand your visibility so new people continuously find your brand and begin engaging with your content.

Stage 2: Generate Leads – Capturing the Attention of Interested Potential Clients

Visibility alone isn't enough. You need to turn casual followers into engaged leads who enter your ecosystem and express interest in learning more from you. This stage is about offering something of value that encourages potential clients to take the next step in building a relationship with you.

Ways to Generate Leads

- **Lead Magnets (Free Resources):** Offering free PDFs, checklists, webinars, or mini-courses in exchange for an email address.
- **Exclusive Communities:** Creating a private Facebook group, WhatsApp community, or membership space where you nurture leads.
- **Quizzes and Assessments:** Interactive tools that help potential clients learn something about themselves while joining your list.
- **Low-Ticket Offers (Tripwires):** Small, entry-level paid products that allow clients to experience your work before committing to higher-ticket offers.

The Goal: Move potential clients from passive observers to engaged, interested leads who are inside your world and open to learning from you.

Stage 3: Nurture Leads – Deepening Trust and Strengthening Relationships

Many entrepreneurs focus heavily on lead generation but struggle to convert those leads into paying clients. That's because trust and relationship-building happen between the moment someone discovers you and the moment they feel ready to invest. The nurturing phase is about building credibility, authority, and connection so that your leads see you as the right person to help them.

Ways to Nurture Leads Effectively

- **Email Sequences and Newsletters:** Sending regular, high-value emails that educate, inspire, and keep you top of mind.
- **Storytelling and Transparency:** Sharing your experience, case studies, and insights to help leads connect with your brand on a deeper level.
- **Live Q&A Sessions and Workshops:** Providing opportunities for leads to interact with you, ask questions, and experience your expertise firsthand.

- **Consistent Content and Engagement:** Keeping your brand present through social media, podcasts, and videos that reinforce your message.

The Goal: Help potential clients feel confident, connected, and ready to take the next step with you.

Stage 4: Convert Leads to Sales – Guiding Them Toward a Confident Purchase Decision

When leads are nurtured properly, selling becomes effortless and natural rather than pushy or forced. This phase is about clearly presenting your offer, overcoming objections, and making it easy for clients to say yes with confidence.

Key Elements of a Strong Conversion Strategy

- **Clear and Compelling Offers:** Clearly communicate the value, transformation, and outcomes of your offer.
- **Sales Pages and Calls to Action:** Make it easy for potential clients to take the next step with well-structured sales pages and invitations to book calls.
- **Launches and Promotions:** Run live launches, challenges, or time-sensitive promotions that create excitement and urgency.
- **Testimonials and Social Proof:** Showcase client success stories and case studies to reinforce credibility.
- **Personalized Follow-Ups:** Reach out to leads who have expressed interest but haven't yet made a decision.

The Goal: Make the decision process clear, easy, and exciting for potential clients so they confidently invest in your offer.

Each stage of this funnel may look different depending on your business model and the offer you are leading people toward. Being clear about your client journey allows you to create intentional marketing touchpoints that move people through this process effectively.

The More Impactfully You Move People Through the Journey, the Faster You Convert

Many entrepreneurs experience slow or inconsistent sales because they are not intentionally guiding their audience through the client journey. If you only focus on creating awareness but don't nurture those leads or guide them to an offer, they remain passive observers rather than engaged buyers.

By designing an aligned marketing pathway that intentionally and strategically moves people from awareness to trust to purchase, you accelerate the client journey in a way that feels natural and organic. The more clarity and consistency you bring to your marketing, the more aligned people will move toward working with you.

Remember, marketing is not about selling. It is about creating a clear pathway for the right people to find you, connect with you, and confidently say yes to working with you. When done with intention, marketing feels less like a chore and more like a natural extension of your work, allowing you to show up authentically and magnetically attract those you are meant to serve.

By mapping out your marketing activities with precision and aligning them with the Know, Like, and Trust process, you create a sustainable and effective strategy that moves people through the client journey seamlessly. The next step is to explore the different marketing channels and strategies that align best with your energy and business goals, which we will dive into in the following sections.

Choosing the Right Pathways

To successfully guide people through your marketing funnel, you must be clear about where you are leading them and choose marketing activities that naturally fit your strengths and your ideal clients' behaviors. Key considerations include the following:

- **In-Person Versus Online:** Are you engaging through networking, speaking, and live events, or are you leveraging digital platforms like social media, email, and content marketing?

- **Free Versus Paid Marketing:** Are you focusing on organic reach through word-of-mouth, free content, and community building, or are you using paid advertising, sponsorships, and collaborations to increase your reach?
- **Marketing Activities:** Which methods feel the most aligned for you and your audience? Some common approaches:
  - Digital downloads (PDF guides, checklists, e-books) to generate leads
  - Webinars, workshops, and master classes to nurture engagement
  - Attending or hosting events to build relationships and authority
  - Networking, collaborations, and referrals for high-trust lead generation
  - Coffee chats, direct messages, and Facebook groups for personal connection
  - Email marketing campaigns to deepen relationships and offer valuable insights
  - Social media content strategies to maintain visibility and engagement
  - Long-form content marketing (blogs, podcasts, YouTube) for authority building

Each of these plays a distinct role in the client journey, so mapping out where and how you communicate at each stage will ensure a cohesive and effective marketing strategy.

Moving People Through Organic Versus Paid Marketing: Finding the Right Balance

A well-rounded marketing strategy includes both organic and paid marketing, each serving a different purpose in attracting, nurturing, and converting leads. Understanding the differences between these two approaches allows you to leverage them strategically based on your business goals, budget, and energetic capacity.

Organic Marketing: Building Relationships and Long-Term Trust

Organic marketing is a relationship-based, content-driven approach that focuses on creating genuine connections, authority, and trust over time. It does not require directly spending money on ads, but it does require consistency and patience to see long-term results.

Benefits of Organic Marketing

- Builds long-term credibility and brand trust
- Attracts highly engaged, aligned clients who resonate with your message
- Requires little to no upfront financial investment
- Strengthens community and deepens relationships with your audience

Common Organic Marketing Strategies

- Content Marketing: Creating valuable, educational, or inspiring content on social media, blogs, YouTube, or podcasts
- SEO: Writing keyword-optimized blog posts and website content to rank in search engines and attract ideal clients passively.
- Social Media Engagement: Showing up consistently, engaging in conversations, and positioning yourself as an expert in your space.
- Networking and Collaborations: Partnering with aligned businesses, appearing on podcasts, or guest speaking to expand your reach organically.
- Referral and Word-of-Mouth Marketing: Encouraging satisfied clients to share their experience and refer new leads.

Best For: entrepreneurs who want to attract warm, engaged clients without relying on ad spend. Great for those who prefer a slow and steady approach that focuses on depth, connection, and long-term brand-building.

Paid Marketing: Accelerating Growth and Scaling Reach

Paid marketing allows your business to increase visibility and generate leads quickly, making it an effective way to reach a larger audience beyond your organically built audience. While organic marketing can take time to build momentum, paid marketing offers a way to accelerate your results by targeting cold audiences who may not have discovered you otherwise.

Benefits of Paid Marketing

- Rapidly increases visibility and lead generation
- Allows precise audience targeting based on interests, behaviors, and demographics
- Helps scale a proven offer by reaching more people in a shorter time
- Creates predictable, measurable results when done correctly

Common Paid Marketing Strategies

- Facebook and Instagram Ads: Running paid promotions to drive traffic to an offer, lead magnet, or webinar
- Google and YouTube Ads: Targeting people actively searching for solutions you provide
- Sponsored Collaborations and Influencer Marketing: Paying for shoutouts, guest appearances, or sponsored posts from influencers in your niche
- Paid Partnerships and Sponsorships: Investing in collaborations with aligned brands, paid podcast sponsorships, or joint venture promotions

Best For: entrepreneurs who want to scale quickly, test offers with a larger audience, or generate leads faster than organic methods allow.

Choosing the Right Approach for Your Business

There is no one-size-fits-all marketing strategy; it depends on your business model, goals, and available resources. Some businesses thrive using purely organic methods, while others see exponential growth through paid marketing. The key is to choose an approach that aligns with your:

- **Business Goals:** Are you focused on long-term brand-building or fast scaling?
- **Budget:** Do you have the financial resources to invest in ads, or are you bootstrapping and relying on free strategies?
- **Energetic Capacity:** Do you enjoy engaging with your audience daily (organic), or do you prefer automation and passive lead generation (paid)?

Many successful entrepreneurs use a hybrid approach, leveraging organic strategies to build trust and community, while incorporating paid strategies to amplify reach and generate leads faster.

A Helpful Marketing Analogy: The Midwife and Birthing Coach

A strong marketing strategy functions like a midwife or birthing coach, meeting people where they are and offering the right support at the right time. The type of marketing that attracts a client is very dependent on where they are in their level of need for your services as well as their awareness that you exist and are able to provide the services they are seeking.

Imagine these different stages:

- **Before Pregnancy:** Educating and supporting women who are considering starting a family. This is like **awareness marketing**, where you provide value to potential clients who are not yet ready to buy.
- **First Trimester:** Helping newly pregnant women navigate early stages. This aligns with **lead nurturing**, providing the right resources to keep people engaged.
- **Second and Third Trimester:** Offering structured guidance as they prepare for birth. This represents **intentional lead conversion**, guiding warm leads into making a buying decision.

- **Post-Birth:** Providing postpartum support. This is **client retention and continued nurturing**, ensuring a positive experience that may lead to referrals and repeat business.

Thinking about your marketing this way ensures that you are not trying to rush people into a decision before they are ready but instead meeting them exactly where they are and guiding them with clarity and care.

Human Design Elements to Consider for Marketing

Marketing is not just about strategy; it's about energy alignment. Visionary entrepreneurs thrive when their marketing aligns with their natural energy, strengths, and way of operating, which is why considering Human Design when creating a marketing plan is so powerful. Instead of forcing themselves into conventional marketing strategies that feel draining or ineffective, Human Design helps them craft a plan that works with their unique energy flow. When marketing is designed in harmony with your Human Design, it becomes a natural extension of your energy, attracting the right clients with more ease and creating momentum without burnout.

Here is how certain parts of your Human Design impact your marketing approach.

Type

This is how your aura interacts with others, and it impacts the way you market your business. Each Human Design Type has a natural way of attracting and engaging clients. Here are aligned marketing examples for each Type:

Manifestors

Best suited for initiating and leading marketing efforts. They thrive with bold, direct messaging and short, high-impact marketing campaigns.

Example: Launching a new offer with an exclusive invitation, creating urgency around new initiatives, or leveraging PR strategies.

Generators

They excel when they respond to interest and engagement. Their marketing should involve consistent content creation, such as blogs, podcasts, or social media interactions where they respond to questions and audience curiosity.

Example: Running a Q&A series, interactive Instagram stories, or responding to audience needs with new offers.

Manifesting Generators

They thrive when combining multiple interests and fast-paced marketing strategies. They do well with multi-channel marketing where they can showcase different aspects of their work.

Example: Hosting live workshops, launching multiple projects simultaneously, and repurposing content across various platforms.

Projectors

They work best when invited into conversations. Their marketing should focus on demonstrating expertise, engaging in thought leadership, and waiting for recognition.

Example: Sharing insights via LinkedIn articles, being featured as a guest expert in interviews, or networking in aligned communities.

Reflectors

They thrive in environments where they can reflect collective needs and trends. Their marketing should be community-focused, allowing them to observe and provide feedback.

Example: Running online community discussions, curating collaborative spaces, or creating content based on current collective themes.

Profile

Your Personality Profile Line determines how people perceive you and what role you naturally embody in your marketing. The way I like to think about this is to really give you clarity on *how* you present yourself because from an energetic perspective, this is what you do best and also what people are seeking from you. When you position yourself in this way, you are highlighting your strengths and thus attracting aligned clients. When you look at your Profile combination (e.g., 1/3), the first number in your Personality Profile is the role that others are looking to you to fulfill for them.

- **Line 1 (The Researcher):** Naturally drawn to research and depth, they excel in marketing through detailed content, educational resources, and thought leadership. Blogs, whitepapers, and in-depth guides resonate well with their audience.
- **Line 2 (The Natural):** They prefer organic attraction rather than forceful marketing. They work best when showcasing natural talent through demonstrations, word-of-mouth, and aligned referrals. Video content and behind-the-scenes sharing can be highly effective.
- **Line 3 (The Experimenter):** They learn best through trial and error, making their marketing most effective when sharing personal experiences, case studies, and lessons learned. Relatable storytelling and vulnerability make them magnetic to their audience.
- **Line 4 (The Connector):** They thrive in relationship-based marketing. Networking, collaborations, and community-driven strategies work best. Leveraging personal connections and social engagement creates the highest impact.
- **Line 5 (The Problem-Solver):** They are naturally seen as a problem-solver and guide, making educational marketing, direct calls to action, and high-value offers particularly effective. Webinars, master classes, and solution-oriented messaging perform well.
- **Line 6 (The Role Model):** They move through different marketing phases: experimentation, reflection, and embodi-

ment. In later life stages, they are most effective as visionary leaders, using authority-based content, mentorship, and legacy-building strategies to attract their audience.

Environment

This is the vibe or setting in which you thrive, and thus directly affects how you show up energetically in your marketing. Your audience will pick up on your energetic alignment, making Environment an important factor. Here are aligned marketing examples based on different Human Design Environments:

- **Markets:** People with this environment thrive in dynamic, ever-changing spaces where trends and opportunities shift quickly. Best marketing activities include attending live events, networking, running sales-driven campaigns, and leveraging fast-paced social media like Instagram and TikTok.
- **Caves:** People with this environment feel best in controlled, intimate spaces. Ideal marketing includes private communities (e.g., exclusive Facebook or WhatsApp groups), VIP experiences, and invite-only masterminds that foster deep, close connections.
- **Shores:** People with this environment enjoy balancing connection and solitude, making it ideal for blending live interactions and prerecorded content. Works well with hybrid events, storytelling-based marketing, and bridging online and offline experiences through webinars, podcasts, and workshops.
- **Kitchens:** People with this environment thrive in collaborative and creative environments, making coworking, community-led projects, and interactive content (like livestream Q&As, collaborative workshops, and behind-the-scenes storytelling) ideal marketing strategies.
- **Valleys:** People with this environment enjoy connection and community-driven marketing. They thrive with group coaching, in-person events, networking, and social media strategies that emphasize two-way engagement, such as LinkedIn conversations, live discussions, and referral-based marketing.

- **Mountains:** People with this environment prefer a higher perspective, making them ideal for long-form content such as blogs, whitepapers, high-level consulting offers, and thought leadership pieces. Prerecorded courses or slow-paced, intentional marketing work well.

Strategy and Authority

Understanding and trusting your Strategy and Authority are the most important aspects of decision-making in your business, especially in marketing. When you rely on external trends or strategies that don't align with your natural energy, you may experience resistance, burnout, or ineffective results. Your Strategy determines how you are meant to engage with the world and initiate opportunities, while your Authority helps you discern which opportunities are correct for you.

These serve as your personal compass, guiding you toward the right actions at the right time, ensuring that every marketing move you make is aligned with your energy and business goals.

Marketing should feel aligned, sustainable, and authentic, not like a forced strategy that drains your energy.

Understanding Strategy in Marketing

Your Human Design Strategy outlines the most effective way for you to take action and engage with opportunities in your business, including how you approach marketing. By aligning with your Strategy, you avoid resistance, burnout, and wasted effort while attracting the right clients with ease.

The Four Human Design Strategies and Their Marketing Approaches

Generators and Manifesting Generators – Strategy: Responding

How This Impacts Marketing: Instead of forcing a marketing plan based on trends or external pressure, Generators and MGs should focus on responding to what excites them and what their audience is already engaging with.

Aligned Marketing Approach

- Pay attention to questions and comments from your audience and create content in response.
- Use engagement-driven marketing, such as polls, Q&As, and interactive content, to see what resonates before committing.
- Notice what excites your Sacral response; if a marketing idea feels heavy, it's not the right path.

Projectors – Strategy: Waiting for the Invitation

How This Impacts Marketing: Projectors thrive when they share their wisdom in a way that invites others in, rather than chasing visibility or pushing their message.

Aligned Marketing Approach

- Position yourself as an authority by sharing deep insights through content (blogging, podcasting, YouTube).
- Focusing on high-value relationships, networking, guest speaking, and collaborations will create more success than mass marketing.
- Recognize when you feel invited to speak on a topic (e.g., if people frequently ask for your take on something, that's a sign to create content around it).

Manifestors – Strategy: Initiating and Informing

How This Impacts Marketing: Manifestors are natural leaders and disruptors, so their marketing should focus on bold action and letting their audience know what they're doing.

Aligned Marketing Approach

- Don't wait for validation; if you feel inspired by an idea, go for it and announce it to your audience.
- Leverage high-impact launches, bold messaging, and independent projects where you set the direction. Use marketing that builds momentum, such as pre-launch announcements, waitlists, and surprise offers.

Reflectors – Strategy: Waiting a Lunar Cycle (28 Days)

How This Impacts Marketing: Reflectors are highly sensitive to energy and need time to feel into the right marketing approach. Rushing decisions can lead to misalignment.

Aligned Marketing Approach

- Give yourself time to test different marketing strategies before committing.
- Focus on community-driven marketing, such as group memberships, collective conversations, and cocreation with others.
- Allow flexibility in your marketing. Remember, your energy shifts, so your approach may as well!

Understanding Authority in Marketing Decisions

Your Authority determines how you make decisions, which is essential when structuring a marketing plan. Instead of choosing tactics based on trends or pressure, you can use your Authority to determine what feels right for you.

The Seven Human Design Authorities and Their Marketing Approach

Sacral Authority – Follow the Excitement

How This Impacts Marketing: Your gut response tells you whether a marketing idea is right for you. If something feels like a drain, don't force it!

Aligned Marketing

- Tune into your Sacral yes/no when planning campaigns; if you feel any resistance in your body, you either need more information, a tweak, or it's a no.
- Engage in real-time marketing, responding to audience questions and trends that light you up.
- Use body-based responses (like saying ideas out loud) to test if a strategy excites you.

Emotional Authority – Wait for Clarity

How This Impacts Marketing: Emotional Authority requires waiting through emotional highs and lows before making marketing decisions.

Aligned Marketing

- Don't rush into big marketing commitments; sleep on ideas before deciding.
- Notice how you feel about marketing strategies over time, not just in the moment.
- Avoid impulsive launches or last-minute pivots; clarity comes with patience.

Splenic Authority – Trust Instant Intuition

How This Impacts Marketing: Your spleen gives you instant, intuitive hits on whether a marketing strategy is right for you.

Aligned Marketing

- Follow your first instinct; if an idea doesn't feel right immediately, it's not for you. Don't try to logically convince yourself otherwise.
- Avoid overthinking or seeking external validation; trust your inner knowing.
- Prioritize quick, instinctive marketing decisions; trust that what feels right now is the right path.

Ego Authority – Lead with Desire

How This Impacts Marketing: If a marketing decision fuels your personal desire and motivation, it's aligned.

Aligned Marketing

- Choose strategies that feel empowering and self-led, not ones that require external permission.
- Follow marketing that allows you to lead confidently—activities like public speaking, brand-building, and bold messaging work well.

- Don't limit yourself by avoiding things because you feel selfish or bad for doing them. This is old conditioning.

Self-Projected Authority – Speak It Out Loud

How This Impacts Marketing: Clarity comes when you talk through ideas and hear yourself express them.

Aligned Marketing

- Use voice-based marketing like podcasts, speaking engagements, or live storytelling.
- Test marketing ideas by talking them out with a trusted sounding board.
- Speak ideas into an AI tool that can convert this into a more thoughtfully organized strategy.

Mental/Environmental Authority – Find the Right Space

How This Impacts Marketing: You need the right physical environment to make good marketing decisions.

Aligned Marketing

- Change your surroundings (e.g., go to a café or in nature) when making big marketing plans.
- Work in a space that feels inspiring; your best marketing ideas will flow in the right setting.
- Ensure the environment in which you are recording video or creating marketing content is inspiring and fuels your creativity.

Lunar Authority – Wait a Full Cycle

How This Impacts Marketing: Reflectors need time to move through all phases of decision-making before committing to marketing strategies.

Aligned Marketing

- Avoid rushing into big marketing plans; wait a full month to see if something still feels right.

- Use trial-and-error marketing that allows for flexibility and evolution.
- Redo past marketing activities that felt good or repurpose past content that you created.

By deeply understanding how your Strategy and Authority operate in real-time, you can create aligned marketing plans with confidence, knowing that every move is energetically aligned rather than based on fear, urgency, or comparison. This means you can trust yourself to make decisions about launching offers, pricing, content creation, and engagement strategies, rather than second-guessing or following someone else's blueprint. The more you lean into your Strategy and Authority, the more magnetic and effortless your marketing becomes.

Practical Application Exercise: Mapping Out Your Marketing Funnel

Mapping out your funnel with intention ensures that every step of your marketing strategy is aligned, effective, and designed to guide your audience through a seamless client journey. A well-structured funnel moves people from initial awareness to becoming loyal, engaged clients. Follow these steps to create an aligned funnel that supports both your business goals and your audience's needs:

1. **Define Your End Goal:** Start with clarity on the primary offer you are leading people toward. Is it a one-on-one service, a group program, a course, or a membership? Knowing your core offer helps shape the steps leading up to it.

2. **Identify Where Your Audience Is Now:** Consider where potential clients currently are in their journey. Are they completely new to you and need awareness-building content? Have they engaged with you but need nurturing before making a decision? Understanding this ensures you tailor your marketing accordingly.

3. **Choose the Right Marketing Activities:** Select two to three marketing strategies that align with your Human Design, strengths, and audience behavior. These might include social media content, networking, email marketing, or

speaking engagements. Ensure that each activity moves people naturally through the Know, Like, and Trust process.

4. **Create Intentional Pathways for Engagement:** Design clear steps that guide your audience deeper into your world. For example:

    • **Awareness Stage:** Social media posts, guest podcasting, SEO blog content

    • **Engagement Stage:** Webinars, free guides, lead magnets, live Q&As

    • **Nurture Stage:** Email sequences, community building, personal outreach

    • **Conversion Stage:** Sales calls, limited-time offers, launch campaigns

5. **Map Out a Timeline for Implementation:** Set up a structured marketing plan with key dates for content releases, lead-generation activities, and conversion-focused efforts. This helps maintain consistency and ensures you aren't relying on random bursts of marketing.

6. **Test, Refine, and Optimize:** Marketing is an evolutionary process. Track what works, refine what doesn't, and adjust your approach based on engagement, conversion rates, and overall resonance with your audience.

By taking the time to map out your marketing funnel with intention, you create a system that feels aligned, supports your energy, and effectively converts your audience into long-term clients.

Common Mistakes to Avoid

Avoiding common mistakes in marketing is crucial for maintaining energetic alignment and effectiveness. Here are some pitfalls that many entrepreneurs face:

    • **Forcing Yourself into Marketing Strategies That Drain You:** When you engage in marketing methods that don't align with your energy or Human Design, it often leads to burnout, inconsistency, or frustration. For example, if you are a

Projector and try to initiate cold sales without waiting for recognition, it can feel exhausting and unproductive. Instead, lean into the strategies that feel most natural and enjoyable for you.

- **Not Marketing Enough Due to Fear of Being Pushy:** Many spiritual entrepreneurs avoid marketing themselves because they don't want to seem too salesy or intrusive. However, if people don't know what you offer, they can't make the decision to work with you. Reframe marketing as an opportunity to educate and invite rather than pressure. You're providing value and allowing people to choose what resonates with them.

- **Not Taking People Through the Full Client Journey:** Marketing is not just about getting people to see you; it's about guiding them step-by-step through the process of awareness, engagement, and conversion. Many business owners focus too much on visibility (posting on social media) but fail to nurture leads or provide clear calls to action that move them into deeper engagement and eventually to a sale.

- **Lacking Consistency or Structure in Your Marketing:** Randomly posting content without a clear strategy creates confusion for your audience. Instead, map out an intentional marketing funnel where every activity serves a specific purpose in moving people from awareness to purchase. This ensures you are building momentum rather than engaging in sporadic marketing efforts that don't yield results.

By being mindful of these mistakes and making intentional, aligned choices, you can create a marketing strategy that feels good, supports your energy, and effectively attracts your ideal clients.

CHAPTER 9

MESSAGING PILLARS: YOUR INTENTIONAL BRAND COMMUNICATION

What Is Messaging?

Messaging is the strategic communication that defines how a brand, business, or individual conveys its values, mission, unique value proposition, and offers to its target audience at different stages of the client journey. It serves as the bridge between what you do and how you make others understand the depth of your work. Effective messaging ensures that you are speaking to the right people in a way that resonates with them, aligns with your business vision, and ultimately leads to conversions.

At its core, messaging answers three fundamental questions:

1. **What are you saying?** Your messaging pillars, which are the core themes or key messages that repeatedly show up in your brand communication.
2. **Who are you saying it to?** This depends on the stage of awareness your audience is in, whether they are just

discovering you, evaluating their options, or ready to make an investment.

3. **Where are you saying it?** The platforms and methods you choose to communicate, including social media, email marketing, website content, or direct conversations.

Your messaging isn't just about broadcasting information; it's about intentionality. Every word you put out into the world should have a purpose and be designed to move potential clients through their journey with you.

The Purpose of Messaging

Messaging isn't just about expressing your brand's voice; it's about moving people closer to key decision points in their journey with you. These decisions might include the following:

- Choosing to follow you on social media
- Subscribing to your email list
- Engaging with your content
- Signing up for a free resource
- Booking a discovery call
- Making a purchase

When your messaging is clear, compelling, and aligned with your business, you naturally attract the right people and make their decision-making process easier. Without strategic messaging, you risk speaking to the wrong audience, using ineffective language, or failing to connect in a meaningful way.

Why Clear and Aligned Messaging Matters

Messaging isn't just nice to have, it's a fundamental part of building a sustainable, aligned business. Without clarity in messaging, entrepreneurs often find themselves:

- **Wasting time talking to the wrong people:** Without strategic messaging, you might attract people who aren't aligned with your offer, leading to frustration and burnout.

- **Feeling like you have to convince people:** If your messaging isn't clear, you may find yourself in a cycle of convincing rather than naturally attracting those who are already seeking what you offer.
- **Experiencing resistance and misalignment:** When your messaging doesn't align with your energy and business vision, it can feel forced and unnatural.

Instead of simply putting content out and hoping it resonates, intentional messaging allows you to focus on four key objectives:

1. **Sharing Your Values and Mission:** Your audience wants to connect with you on a deeper level. By consistently communicating your values, you attract people who align with your vision and purpose.
2. **Providing Value:** Thoughtful messaging allows you to educate, inspire, and support your audience before they ever invest in your offers.
3. **Clearly Communicating What You Do:** Ambiguity is one of the biggest barriers to client conversion. Messaging ensures that people understand what you offer, how you can help, and why they should trust you.
4. **Helping Clients Self-Identify If They Are Right for You:** Effective messaging allows potential clients to see themselves in your work, naturally filtering those who are the best fit for your offers.

Many of the clients I have worked with shared with me that they thought their messaging was off and that was why they were not getting clients. I remember working with an energy healer and practitioner who said her niche was moms struggling with burnout and her work would help them find relief. Diving deeper into her Human Design chart, I could see that as a 1/3 Generator with the Right Angle Cross of Consciousness, her messaging and lack of clients was a symptom of underlying misalignment in her business. This woman had gone through a profound change in her own life, shifting from a very religious background to having a spiritual awakening that altered how she was living her own life. Yet her offers were not spiritual at all, and she was hiding this part of her, which was a *huge* part of her current identity and how she actually served her clients in her business. When I showed her that her messaging was off because she was not sharing about the real work she did with clients in her services, she saw it wasn't a messaging issue, it was an alignment issue. Her old messaging was about burnout and her new messaging was about awakening. Want to know what happened to her business after that? New offers, new clients, and a whole new sense of alignment poured in.

By refining your messaging pillars, aligning them with the right audience, and strategically choosing where to share them, you set yourself up for a business that flows effortlessly, attracting the right clients with ease.

Business Elements of Messaging

Messaging is the foundation of how your business communicates its value, mission, and unique approach to the world. It's more than just words; it's the energy behind how you attract, engage, and convert your ideal clients. Without clear, aligned messaging, even the best offers can go unnoticed or misunderstood. In this section, we'll explore the essential business elements of messaging, how to craft a compelling brand voice, define your core message, and communicate in a way that resonates with the right audience. Whether you're writing social media content, sales pages, or client emails, understanding these core elements will help you create messaging that feels authentic, magnetic, and strategically effective for business growth.

Communicating a Clear Client Journey

Your messaging should always guide your audience toward a clear next step. Every piece of content, email, social media post, or conversation should be intentional in leading potential clients closer to working with you. The key objectives include the following:

- **Developing Greater Awareness:** Positioning yourself as the solution to your audience's core problems or desires, ensuring they understand what you offer and why it matters.
- **Offering Lead Magnets and Introductory Resources:** Free resources like e-books, webinars, or templates help nurture potential clients and introduce them to your methodology.
- **Directing Toward Paid Offers:** Whether it's a low-cost product, a discovery call, or a signature program, your messaging should strategically move leads from awareness to action.

Defining Your Messaging Pillars

Your messaging pillars form the foundation of your brand communication. These are the key themes you continuously emphasize across all your platforms and interactions to establish consistency and authority. Effective messaging pillars include the following:

- **Core Values and Mission:** What principles guide your business, and what transformation do you help clients achieve?
- **Educational Content:** Teach your audience about your niche, industry insights, and the foundational knowledge they need to succeed.
- **Personal Stories and Authenticity:** Infuse personal experiences and real-life testimonials to build connection and trust.
- **Call to Action and Offers:** Clearly and confidently state what you offer and how it can help, ensuring that your audience understands their next step.

Stages of Awareness

To communicate effectively, you must understand where your audience is in their journey and tailor your messaging accordingly. The key stages of awareness include the following:

- **Symptom Awareness:** The client recognizes they have a challenge or an unfulfilled desire but may not fully understand the root cause. Messaging should focus on highlighting the problem and validating their experience.
- **Problem Awareness:** The client now understands their specific problem and is seeking a solution. At this stage, messaging should educate them on why solving the problem is important and introduce possible solutions.
- **Solution Awareness:** The client is actively looking for the right offer or service to address their need. Messaging should emphasize why your solution is the best choice, differentiating it from competitors and guiding them toward action.

By aligning content with these stages, you create a seamless journey that naturally leads potential clients to trust and invest in your business.

Benefits Versus Features

A critical mistake many entrepreneurs make is focusing too much on features instead of benefits. While features provide necessary details, benefits showcase transformation and emotional appeal. Here's how to differentiate the two:

- **Benefits:** Focus on how your product or service directly solves pain points and improves your client's life. These should evoke emotion and highlight transformation. Example: Gain clarity and confidence in your business strategy so you can scale with ease.
- **Features:** These are the tangible elements of your offer, such as "Eight weeks of coaching," "Lifetime access," or "Step-by-step modules." While necessary, they should support, not lead, your messaging.

By leading with benefits and backing them up with features, you create messaging that is both compelling and practical, making it easier for potential clients to say yes to your offers.

Human Design Elements for Messaging

Understanding your messaging through the lens of Human Design allows you to communicate in alignment with your natural energy, ensuring that your words resonate deeply with your ideal audience. Instead of relying solely on traditional marketing logic, this approach taps into your unique energetic blueprint, allowing for more authentic, magnetic, and impactful messaging.

What Are You Talking About?

In business, we are here to solve problems or fulfill desires. Often, we focus on logical aspects when we communicate about our business, but Human Design provides insight into key aspects of our chart that, when integrated into our messaging, activate a higher frequency. This allows us to operate from a place of flow and magnetism rather than force and resistance.

- **Incarnation Cross:** This represents your life purpose and overarching themes in your messaging. Your core mission and the lessons you are meant to teach can form the foundation of your messaging pillars. This is your natural role in the world, and when you weave it into your messaging, you create deeper resonance. For example:
  - **Right Angle Cross** often centers around personal transformation, so messaging should highlight individual growth.
  - **Left Angle Cross** is about shared experiences and collective evolution, making community-driven messaging more effective.
  - **Juxtaposition Cross** combines stability with change, requiring messaging that balances personal authority with flexibility.
- **Shadows of Your Sun Gates:** The challenges associated with your Sun Gates often mirror the struggles of your ideal clients.

By authentically sharing your journey through these challenges and how you've embodied their higher frequencies, you create trust, relatability, and authority. When you acknowledge and share the shadows of these gates, you create a connection point for your audience. This builds trust and allows others to see themselves in your journey.

How Are You Talking About It?

How you express your message matters just as much as what you're saying. The way you communicate your message is just as critical as the message itself. In Human Design, the way you speak, share, and express your ideas is determined by key energetic aspects of your chart. These elements help you align your communication style with your natural strengths, making your message more compelling and resonant.

Your Human Design provides clues about the most aligned way for you to communicate:

- **Profile:** Your profile represents the personality that people are naturally drawn to. Understanding your Profile helps you lean into your strengths and communicate in a way that naturally attracts the right clients.
- **Conscious Mercury Gate:** Mercury represents communication and the energy with which you naturally express yourself. Identifying your conscious Mercury Gate reveals the specific approach you should take in messaging, whether it's storytelling, direct guidance, or innovation-driven teaching.
- **Throat Center:** The Throat Center in Human Design governs communication and self-expression. Whether your Throat Center is defined or undefined influences how you naturally share your message and how your audience perceives you:
  - Defined Throat Center: If your Throat Center is defined, you have consistent access to your voice and message. You may find it easier to articulate your ideas and feel a natural flow in communication. Your messaging benefits

from structure and clarity, as your words carry weight and influence.

- Undefined or Open Throat Center: If your Throat Center is undefined, your communication style is more fluid and influenced by your environment. You may express yourself differently depending on who you are around. This makes storytelling and adaptability key strengths, but you may need to cultivate consistency in your messaging.

The Throat Gates and Their Messaging Influence

The Throat Center in Human Design is the hub of communication and manifestation; it's how we express our ideas, share our insights, and bring thoughts into the world. Each of these gates in this center influences how a person naturally communicates, the energy behind their words, and the way their messaging resonates with others. Whether speaking, writing, or presenting, understanding your activated Throat Gates can help you craft messaging that feels authentic, aligned, and impactful.

Below is a breakdown of each Throat Gate and how it shapes your communication style:

Gate 62 (The Gate of Details) – The Logical Communicator

- This gate thrives on structured, fact-based, and precise messaging.
- Messaging should focus on breaking down complex ideas into logical, digestible pieces.
- People with this gate activated excel at teaching, organizing, and presenting factual evidence in a way that makes sense.
- Best Used In: Data-driven content, educational materials, step-by-step frameworks, and well-organized presentations. It is important to use precision and clarity in your communication when you have this gate defined.

Gate 23 (The Gate of Assimilation) – The Simplifier

- This gate has the gift of taking complex or abstract concepts and expressing them in a way that is easy to understand.
- Messaging should be clear, innovative, and insightful, avoiding unnecessary complexity.
- Often, people with this gate receive sudden downloads of knowledge and must trust their ability to explain things in a way that clicks for others.
- Best Used In: Thought leadership, innovation-driven messaging, simplifying high-level ideas, and bringing fresh perspectives to the table.

Gate 56 (The Gate of Storytelling) – The Narrative Messenger

- This is the gate of captivating stories, engaging narratives, and emotional resonance.
- Messaging should be rich with anecdotes, metaphors, and personal experiences to make content more relatable and memorable.
- People with this gate activated can pull audiences in with their words and make complex topics come alive.
- Best Used In: Brand storytelling, public speaking, content marketing, and personal brand building. Be sure to use storytelling and authentic, expressive communication if you have this gate defined.

Gate 35 (The Gate of Change and Experience) – The Transformation Speaker

- This gate speaks from experience, transformation, and personal evolution.
- Messaging should highlight growth journeys, before-and-after stories, and the wisdom gained through experience.
- These individuals often inspire others by showing what's possible through real-life stories of progress and change.
- Best Used In: Coaching businesses, personal development messaging, motivational content, and storytelling that

demonstrates change. Be sure to share your personal experiences if you have this gate defined.

Gate 12 (The Gate of Caution) – The Selective Speaker

- This gate speaks only when the timing feels right, meaning messaging should be deliberate, impactful, and emotionally charged.
- People with this gate often have a dramatic or poetic way of speaking that deeply influences their audience.
- Messaging should be carefully curated, ensuring that each word holds weight and significance.
- Best Used In: Emotional storytelling, persuasive speaking, poetry, and artistic or soulful messaging. Infuse emotions and intentional connections to your clients' outcomes if you have this gate defined.

Gate 33 (The Gate of Privacy and Reflection) – The Wisdom Keeper

- This gate is about retreating, reflecting, and then sharing wisdom when the time is right.
- Messaging should come from deep introspection, personal experiences, and learned lessons.
- People with this gate activated often prefer to process experiences first before sharing their insights with the world.
- Best Used In: Reflective writing, memoirs, legacy-driven content, and deeply insightful messaging.

Gate 45 (The Gate of Leadership and Resources) – The Wealth Messenger

- This gate speaks with authority about leadership, financial empowerment, and resource management.
- Messaging should position the speaker as a confident leader, mentor, or authority in their industry.

- People with this gate command respect through their words and naturally lead others toward financial and strategic empowerment.
- Best Used In: Thought leadership, business coaching, wealth consciousness messaging, and high-level brand positioning. Your communication should express authority and showcase resource management in your messaging.

Gate 31 (The Gate of Influence) – The Visionary Leader

- This is the voice of the collective, guiding others through insightful leadership and forward-thinking vision.
- Messaging should be inspirational, future-focused, and positioned to shape industries or movements.
- People with this gate have a natural ability to influence and rally others toward big-picture change.
- Best Used In: Establishing leadership, visionary brand messaging, movement-building, and audience leadership. Be sure to provide examples of your visionary leadership in your communication.

Gate 20 (The Gate of Now) – The Immediate Messenger

- This gate is all about spontaneous, in-the-moment expression.
- Messaging should be direct, immediate, and focused on present energy, rather than pre-planned or scripted content.
- People with this gate speak with clarity and presence, drawing attention with their raw, unscripted delivery.
- Best Used In: Live speaking, social media stories, unscripted video content, and real-time engagement. Focus on creating content and messaging in the present moment to powerfully communicate at an energetic level.

Gate 16 (The Gate of Skills and Enthusiasm) – The Passionate Communicator

- This gate expresses itself through passion, expertise, and enthusiasm.

- Messaging should showcase mastery in a skill or topic, engaging audiences through sheer excitement and deep knowledge.
- People with this gate activated have a magnetic energy when speaking about their area of expertise.
- Best Used In: Public speaking, brand storytelling, sales presentations, and any messaging that requires energy and expertise. The frequency and energy that you communicate with are vital to your effective communication.

Gate 8 (The Gate of Contribution and Creative Influence) – The Inspired Influencer

- This gate expresses itself through offering unique ideas, creative input, and contributions that shape the direction of others.
- Messaging should highlight originality, personal perspective, and how your vision or creations add value to a larger collective.
- People with this gate activated have a natural gift for influencing trends, inspiring others, and positioning themselves as those whose contributions matter.
- Best Used In: Thought-leadership content, social media influence, creative collaborations, and any messaging that calls others to rally behind your vision. Be sure to use future-focused and inspirational messaging in your communication.

By aligning your messaging with your Human Design, you move beyond generic marketing strategies and create an authentic, magnetic presence that attracts the right people with ease and clarity.

Practical Application Exercise: Identifying Your Messaging Pillars Through Human Design

To create messaging that is deeply aligned with your unique Human Design, follow these steps to identify and refine your core messaging pillars:

Step 1: Identify Your Core Themes

Your messaging should be built on themes that are rooted in your Human Design chart. Explore these key aspects:

- **Incarnation Cross:** What overarching themes and purpose does your Incarnation Cross indicate?
- **Conscious Mercury Gate:** What specific lens or perspective does your Mercury Gate give to your communication?
- **Defined Centers (especially the Throat Center):** If defined, how can you leverage your natural ability to communicate? If undefined, how can you refine your adaptability in expression?
- **Profile Lines:** How do your Profile Lines inform your communication style and how your audience perceives you?

Step 2: Align Your Themes with Your Audience's Awareness Stages

To ensure your messaging is effective, match your Human Design themes to different levels of audience awareness:

- **Symptom Awareness:** How does your messaging validate their current challenges or desires?
- **Problem Awareness:** How does your messaging help them identify and understand their problem?
- **Solution Awareness:** How does your messaging showcase you as the best solution to potential clients' needs?

Step 3: Create Your Messaging Pillars

Your messaging pillars are the recurring themes that establish your expertise and attract your ideal clients. Using insights from Step 1, define three to five core messaging pillars, such as:

- **Transformation and Results:** Showcasing client success and the tangible outcomes of your work
- **Your Unique Methodology:** Explaining how your approach is distinct and effective

- **Personal Connection and Storytelling:** Sharing experiences that make your brand relatable
- **Empowerment and Action:** Encouraging clients to take the next step with confidence
- **Education and Thought Leadership:** Positioning yourself as an authority in your field

Step 4: Develop Content Prompts for Each Pillar

To ensure consistency in your messaging, create content prompts that align with each of your messaging pillars. Examples include the following:

- What does my Incarnation Cross reveal about my business mission, and how can I communicate that to my audience?
- How can I integrate my Conscious Mercury Gate into my messaging to create deeper resonance?
- What personal experiences align with my Vocation Sphere that I can use to inspire my audience?

Step 5: Implement and Refine

Once your messaging pillars and content prompts are established, begin integrating them into your social media, emails, website, and offers. Continuously refine based on audience engagement and feedback.

By using this practical exercise, you ensure that your messaging is authentic, impactful, and aligned with your unique energetic blueprint, making it easier to attract and convert the right clients.

Common Mistakes to Avoid

Avoiding common messaging pitfalls ensures that your communication remains clear, compelling, and aligned with your Human Design. Yes, there are more here than in any other category because the words you speak are immensely powerful. Here are key mistakes to watch out for:

- **Talking Without Intention or Strategy:** Randomly posting content without a clear objective can confuse your audience. Each message should serve a purpose in moving potential clients through their decision-making journey.

- **Ignoring Audience Awareness Stages:** Failing to tailor your messaging to where your audience is in their journey (symptom, problem, or solution awareness) leads to misalignment. Speak to their level of understanding to build trust.

- **Not Conducting Market Research:** Messaging that doesn't incorporate the exact language and pain points your audience uses can result in a disconnect. Conduct interviews, surveys, or social listening to ensure your words resonate.

- **Overcomplicating Your Message:** Using jargon or overly complex explanations can alienate potential clients. Keep it simple, clear, and direct so that your audience immediately understands your offer.

- **Failing to Leverage Your Unique Human Design Expression:** Your defined or undefined Throat Center, Conscious Mercury Gate, and Profile shape the most natural way for you to communicate. Not integrating these aspects can make messaging feel forced or inauthentic.

- **Ignoring Storytelling and Emotional Connection:** Facts alone won't sell; people connect through stories and emotions. Share personal experiences and case studies to create relatability.

- **Trying to Speak to Everyone:** A message that tries to appeal to everyone resonates with no one. Clarify your niche and ideal audience to make your messaging more powerful and targeted.

By addressing these common mistakes, you ensure that your messaging remains focused, effective, and energetically aligned, making it easier to attract and convert the right clients.

CHAPTER 10

CREATING AN ALIGNED SALES PROCESS

What Is a Sales Process?

At its core, a sales process is simply the journey of turning potential leads or prospects into paying customers. It's how you present your offers in a way that allows people to solve a problem or fulfill a deep desire they have. Sales is often misunderstood, but at its essence, it's about connection, service, and alignment.

There is no single "right" way to sell. Some businesses thrive on formal proposals and structured pitches, while others succeed through casual conversations and organic connections. The key to creating a sustainable, aligned business is designing a sales process that feels natural to you and works with your strengths, rather than forcing yourself into a rigid structure that doesn't fit.

The ability to sell effectively is a skill that can absolutely be developed over time. However, how easily you build this skill is highly dependent on a variety of factors, including but not limited to the following:

- **How you feel about the offer you are selling:** When you deeply believe in the transformation your offer provides, selling becomes an act of service rather than a chore. If you struggle with selling, it may be worth exploring whether you are fully aligned with what you're offering.

- **Your past experiences with selling:** Many entrepreneurs have been conditioned to associate sales with pushy, aggressive tactics, often because of negative experiences with traditional sales approaches. If you've ever felt pressured to buy something, you might subconsciously resist selling because you don't want to make others feel that way.

- **Your own limiting beliefs and self-doubt:** Fears of rejection, feelings of unworthiness, or doubts about your value can create hesitation when it comes time to make an offer. Recognizing and working through these blocks is essential to building a sales process that feels good and gets results.

Rather than seeing sales as something to get better at in the traditional sense, I encourage you to see it as an opportunity to refine your communication, deepen your confidence, and create a seamless bridge between you and the people who need your work the most.

Why an Aligned Sales Process Matters

For your business to thrive, selling must happen. Without sales, there is no revenue, and without revenue, your business cannot grow or sustain itself. Many entrepreneurs start their businesses fueled by passion, wanting to serve and make an impact, but they quickly realize that without a consistent, intentional way to bring in clients, they struggle to create financial stability.

A well-thought-out sales process ensures that revenue flows consistently, making your business sustainable. It doesn't mean you need to adopt traditional, high-pressure sales techniques, but it does mean you need a clear pathway that allows potential clients to step into your world with ease.

However, for many of the entrepreneurs I've worked with, this is the most intimidating component of their business, the part they wish they didn't have to do, the part they often avoid. If this resonates with you, know that you are not alone. Selling can feel deeply uncomfortable, especially if you carry preconceived notions about what sales should look like.

Many people have had negative experiences with sales, pushy tactics, manipulation, or being pressured into something they didn't truly want. If that's your perception of sales, it makes sense that you'd resist it. But what if I told you that sales doesn't have to look like that? What if, instead of seeing it as something to *convince* someone of, you saw it as a natural extension of your work, as a conversation where you guide someone toward an aligned decision? This is possible.

Shifting your perspective on sales is the first step to creating a process that feels authentic to you. Sales isn't about forcing anyone into a decision; it's about inviting them into a transformation they already desire. When you see it this way, the discomfort begins to melt away, and selling becomes a natural and aligned part of your business.

Detaching the Visionary from the Business: Selling Without Taking It Personally

One of the biggest shifts of mindset you must embrace as a spiritual entrepreneur is separating yourself, the visionary, from the business itself. This is especially important when it comes to selling because, for many, making an offer feels deeply personal. If you're selling a product, program, or service that is 100 percent delivered by you, it's easy to equate a potential client's decision as a reflection of your worth, expertise, or ability. But this is a distortion that can create unnecessary emotional weight around sales conversations.

Selling is not about proving yourself. It is about extending an invitation. When someone says *yes*, they are not validating your worth. When someone says *no*, they are not rejecting you as a person. Their response is simply information—data that tells you whether your offer is aligned with their current needs, desires, and level of awareness.

Every prospective client is at a different stage in their journey. Some may be fully ready for the transformation you provide, whereas others may need more time, clarity, or experience before they recognize the value of your offer. This is not a reflection of you, it's a reflection of where *they* are.

Understanding Alignment in Sales

Think of sales as a process of discovery, not a performance. When you present your offer, you are essentially asking: *Does what I am offering align with where you are right now and what you desire to create?* Their answer, whether yes or no, is simply an indicator of fit.

When you detach yourself from the outcome, selling becomes much easier because you no longer carry the emotional burden of feeling like you need to convince, prove, or win someone over. Instead, you shift into a space of trust—trust that the right clients will recognize the value of your work and step forward when the timing is aligned.

If someone says no, instead of internalizing it, you can reframe it as:

- This person may not be the right fit for this offer, and that's okay.
- They may need more time or more clarity before they're ready to invest in this transformation.
- Their no has nothing to do with my capabilities or worth; it's simply a reflection of their current priorities and stage of awareness.

By taking this approach, you create a more open, easeful relationship with selling. You are not forcing anything. You are not attaching your identity to an outcome. You are simply presenting an aligned opportunity and allowing others to make the right choice for themselves.

Releasing the Emotional Charge Around *No*

Many entrepreneurs feel discomfort around sales because they fear rejection. But what if rejection isn't actually happening? What if a no is just redirection, a sign that your offer isn't what that person needs *right now?* Or perhaps they need a different solution all together. We need to see these as business decisions, instead of ones that determine our personal value.

When you view sales through this lens, you become more resilient. You no longer see a no as something to take personally, but instead as valuable insight into your audience, your messaging, and the way your offers are positioned. You begin to see patterns, what types of clients say yes immediately, what objections arise most frequently, and how you can refine your approach to better align with those who truly need your work.

This shift allows you to sell with confidence and neutrality, not pushing, not forcing, but standing in your power, knowing that your work holds immense value and that the right people will recognize that when they are ready. Selling, at its highest frequency, is an exchange of alignment. It is not about trying to convince. It is about offering clarity, holding space, and trusting that the right people will step forward when the time is right.

Business Elements Related to Selling

Now that we've explored the mindset of selling and the importance of detaching your identity from the outcome, let's shift into the practical business components of a well-structured sales process. Having a clear, intentional system allows you to sell in a way that feels natural while ensuring consistency and predictability in your revenue.

Understanding the Sales Process

Sales do not happen in a vacuum. Before someone invests in your offer, they typically go through a journey that begins with awareness and moves toward decision-making. Your marketing efforts help generate leads—potential clients who are aware of you and are interested in what you offer. Once those leads are in your world, the sales process begins.

At its simplest, selling involves the following:

1. **Creating interest:** Your marketing efforts attract potential clients who resonate with your work.
2. **Presenting an opportunity:** You directly (through sales calls or DMs) or indirectly (through sales pages or Instagram stories) invite them to take the next step.

3. **Facilitating a decision:** The person makes a choice to invest in your offer or not, based on their needs, desires, and priorities.

When you understand this flow, selling becomes less about forcing an outcome and more about guiding a natural progression, from interest to aligned action.

Sales Frequencies: Launching Versus Evergreen

Different businesses operate on different sales models. Understanding the two primary approaches can help you decide what aligns best with your energy and business strategy.

Launching / Periodic Sales Process

A launch-based sales model involves selling an offer within a scheduled timeframe. There are many different styles of launch, but the main point is that this is an intentional periodic sales cycle.

- **Seasonal:** A program or service that opens for enrollment at specific times of the year.
- **Based on your preferred schedule:** A rhythm you create that supports your business model and energetic flow.

Launching creates urgency, as people know they have a limited time to make a decision. It can be energetically intense, but when done well, it creates excitement and momentum.

Evergreen Sales Process

Evergreen offers are always available for purchase. This model allows people to join whenever they are ready, without waiting for an enrollment period. It provides steady revenue but requires a strong marketing and sales system to ensure consistent visibility.

Choosing between a launch or evergreen model depends on:

- Your Human Design Energy Type and how you prefer to work.
- The nature of your offer (some transformations are better suited for cohorts, while others can be accessed anytime).
- Your personal preference for structured cycles versus ongoing availability.

Examples of Conversion Events

A **conversion event** is any experience that helps a lead transition into a paying client. This could be direct (one-on-one conversation) or indirect (content that guides them toward a decision).

Common examples include the following:

- **Discovery/Sales Calls:** A conversation where you explore the client's needs and see if your offer is the right fit.
- **DM Conversations:** Casual, low-pressure interactions that provide clarity and invite the right people to take action.
- **Workshops and Webinars:** Events that provide value and lead to an intentional offer at the end.
- **Instagram Stories and Social Content:** Subtle but consistent ways to remind your audience about your offer and why it matters.
- **Sales Pages:** A detailed page that presents your offer, speaks to the client's desires, and provides a clear way to buy.
- **Application Process:** This involves the potential client to complete an application form with an acceptance or denial process that determines if they are eligible to join your programs or for your services.

Each of these approaches allows you to create multiple pathways for people to say yes in a way that feels natural to them.

Sales Communications: The Power of Invitation

Sales, at its highest level, is an invitation into transformation. It's not about pushing or pressuring, it's about guiding the right people toward the next step that aligns with their needs, desires, and vision for themselves.

A well-structured sales communication strategy ensures that your audience understands the offer, sees the value, and feels empowered to make a decision. The key elements of effective sales communication include the following:

A Clear Call to Action (CTA)

Every sales message—whether it's in a discovery call, Instagram story, email, or webinar—must have a specific, direct, and clear next step for the person engaging with it. If someone is intrigued but doesn't know what to do next, you risk losing them to confusion or indecision.

A strong call-to-action removes ambiguity and makes it easy for your audience to take the next step. Rather than using vague statements like, "Let me know if you're interested" or "Check out my program," be direct and specific about the action you want them to take. For example, you might say, "Book your free discovery call here" and include a direct link, "Join [program name] today by clicking here," or "Reply with 'I'm in' to start the conversation about working together." Clear, specific CTAs guide your audience with confidence and create a natural pathway into your offers. Clarity removes resistance. If a potential client has to think too hard about what to do next, they may hesitate or drop off entirely.

Making the Invitation Feel Natural and Aligned

One of the biggest mistakes entrepreneurs make in sales is approaching it with a sense of desperation or uncertainty. If you feel uncomfortable making an offer, that energy is felt by your audience.

Instead of seeing sales as getting someone to buy, reframe it as extending a helpful invitation. Think about when you invite a friend to a gathering: You don't force them to come, you simply share the details, the experience they can expect, and let them decide.

The best way to embody this mindset in your messaging is by using inclusive, warm, and confident language:

- "I would love to support you in reaching [desired outcome]. Here's how we can work together."
- "This program is designed for [ideal client]. If this sounds like you, I'd love to invite you in."
- "If this speaks to you, let's chat and see if it's the right fit."

Selling with conviction instead of convincing makes your invitations feel empowered rather than needy, and people naturally respond to confidence and clarity.

Sales Objections: What They Really Mean

Every entrepreneur will face objections during the sales process, but not all objections mean the same thing. Learning to navigate them with confidence ensures that you aren't taking resistance personally, but rather seeing it as an opportunity for deeper understanding.

Can Sales Objections Be Avoided?

Honestly, it depends. There are so many factors that play into sales objections. The better your messaging, positioning, and communication, the fewer objections you'll encounter because the right people will already be pre-aligned before they even reach the decision point.

For example:

- If people are frequently saying, "I'm not sure what's included," your sales page or messaging may not be clear enough.
- If many potential clients say, "I need to think about it," you may not be addressing their biggest fears or hesitations ahead of time.
- If price objections come up often, your value may not be clearly communicated, or you may not be speaking to clients at the right stage of their journey.

Fine-tuning your messaging helps minimize objections, but they may still come up, and that's where mindset and strategy come into play.

Convincing Versus Conviction

There's a big difference between convincing someone to buy and selling with conviction.

- Convincing energy sounds like: "Please say yes," "Let me try to make you see the value," "How can I get you to trust me?"

- Conviction energy sounds like: "This is the right fit for you if…" "I stand behind the power of this offer." "I trust that you will know when the timing is right."

People do not want to be persuaded into a decision, they want to feel empowered in making the right choice for themselves. Your role is to hold the belief in your offer and its value without needing to force a yes.

The Reality of Sales Objections

Some objections are real. If a person genuinely cannot afford an offer or isn't in the right stage of their journey, their *no* is valid.

Other objections are fear-based hesitations disguised as logic. Potential clients might say either:

- "I need to think about it," when they really mean "I'm afraid to invest in myself," or
- "I don't have the time," when they really mean "I'm unsure if I'll fully commit to this."

Your job isn't to override their feelings, but to ask deeper questions that help them uncover what's truly holding them back. Instead of defensively responding to an objection, try:

- "I completely understand. Can I ask what part you're feeling uncertain about?" or
- "Would you like support in working through any hesitations?"

This allows the person to reflect on their own fears and make a more aligned decision.

Payment Options: Creating Accessibility and Flow

Once someone is ready to buy, the sales process should feel seamless and easy. One of the most overlooked elements of selling is offering payment options that meet different financial comfort levels while still honoring the value of your work.

Pay in Full (PIF) Versus Payment Plans: Creating Flexible and Sustainable Investment Options

When you present an offer to potential clients, the way you structure payment options plays a huge role in their decision-making process. Some people prefer the ease of a one-time investment, making the payment and fully committing without thinking about it again. Others need financial flexibility, knowing that breaking payments into smaller, manageable amounts allows them to invest without stress.

Both pay-in-full and payment plan options have distinct advantages, and when structured intentionally, they create a win-win situation, allowing clients to invest in a way that feels good for them while ensuring that your business remains financially sustainable. Understanding the psychology behind these options helps you create an offer that feels accessible, aligned, and supportive for both you and your clients.

Pay-in-Full: The Power of Immediate Commitment

When a client chooses pay-in-full, they are making an energetic and financial commitment up front. There's no lingering decision fatigue and no monthly reminders, just a sense of completion. Many entrepreneurs choose to incentivize this option, offering a small discount or a bonus to reward those who invest fully.

This approach works particularly well for clients who value simplicity and efficiency, they don't want to think about payments later, and they may even feel more invested in their transformation because they made a significant up front decision. A pay-in-full client often moves through a program with more focus, knowing they've made a full commitment from day one. But not everyone is in a position to pay a large sum all at once, and that's where payment plans come in.

Payment Plans: Making Transformation More Accessible

Payment plans open doors. They give potential clients the opportunity to say yes when they might otherwise hesitate. Instead of seeing a high price point and immediately feeling like the offer is out of reach, they can look at a manageable monthly payment and realize, *I can make this work.*

For many, a payment plan is not just about affordability, it's about alignment with their financial flow. Some clients run businesses where income fluctuates, and a structured payment plan helps them feel confident in their ability to commit. Others may simply feel more comfortable with spreading out the investment, giving them peace of mind while still accessing the support they need.

As a business owner, payment plans also create recurring revenue, allowing you to generate predictable income over time. But they do come with their own set of considerations, tracking multiple payments, handling potential failed transactions, and maintaining long-term client engagement. That's why setting clear policies and using automated systems is key to making payment plans work smoothly.

Creating the Right Balance in Your Business

When deciding how to structure payments, it's important to ask the following:

- How does this impact my cash flow?
- What is most supportive for my ideal clients?
- What feels energetically aligned for me as a business owner?

Some offers naturally lend themselves to a PIF-only model, for example, a short-term workshop or a service with a clear, one-time delivery. Others, especially high-ticket coaching or group programs, benefit from both PIF and payment plan options, giving people the ability to choose what works best for them.

The best approach? Intentional choice. Offering both options, structured in a way that supports both you and your clients, creates a sense of ease, accessibility, and sustainability. Those who are ready to commit fully can do so, while those who need a more flexible approach can still step into the transformation you provide.

At the end of the day, payment options should remove barriers, not create them, making it easier for the right clients to say yes in a way that feels fully aligned.

Onboarding: Selling Doesn't End at Payment

Many entrepreneurs make the mistake of thinking that once a sale is made, the process is complete. But onboarding is just as important as selling, because how a client experiences the first steps of working with you directly impacts their satisfaction and results.

Elements of a Strong Onboarding Process

- **Contracts and Agreements**
  - Clearly outline terms, expectations, and boundaries.
  - Reinforce trust by ensuring mutual understanding.

- **Payment Processing and Confirmation**
  - Automate confirmations so clients immediately know their payment went through successfully.
  - Send a welcome email with next steps to prevent post-purchase confusion.

- **Scheduling and Access to Resources**
  - Ensure that clients know exactly what to do next.
  - If applicable, provide links to book calls, access a portal, or begin onboarding materials.

A seamless onboarding experience builds trust, reduces uncertainty, and sets the tone for a powerful client journey.

Selling as an Aligned Process

When you shift your perspective on sales from "getting people to buy" to guiding the right people into alignment, everything changes. The more you trust in your offer, the easier it becomes to communicate your value, navigate objections with ease, and create a sales process that feels aligned, expansive, and empowering.

Human Design Elements in Selling

One of the most empowering aspects of integrating Human Design into business is understanding how your unique energy influences the way you sell. Your sales process should feel natural and aligned with how you are designed to operate, not forced or exhausting.

Many entrepreneurs struggle with sales because they believe they have to follow a traditional, one-size-fits-all approach. But when you design your sales process based on your Human Design Type, Environment, and natural strengths, selling becomes an extension of who you are rather than something you have to force.

How Your Human Design Type Impacts Your Sales Process

Each Human Design Type has its own unique energy flow and structural style that affects how they best engage in sales conversations.

Generators and Manifesting Generators: Selling Through Response

- Your sales process works best when you *respond to interest*, rather than forcing or initiating out of pressure.
- Your excitement and enthusiasm about your offer create a natural magnetism that draws the right people to you.
- If a sales method feels frustrating, it's a sign to tweak the approach until it flows.
- Best sales strategies: Interactive content (polls, questions), live conversations, and responding to client needs in real-time.

Projectors: Selling Through Invitation and Recognition

- Your sales approach should feel *guided and invited*, rather than pushing for the sale.
- People naturally recognize your wisdom, so position yourself as an expert who offers insights, and then wait for the right opportunities.
- If sales feels draining, you may be initiating too much rather than attracting aligned invitations.
- Best sales strategies: Workshops, referrals, in-depth one-on-one sales calls, content that showcases expertise.

Manifestors: Selling Through Bold Initiation

- You are naturally built to *lead* the sales conversation and *create* excitement.
- Your most aligned sales process allows you to speak first and create urgency, without waiting for permission.
- If sales feels misaligned, you may be over-explaining instead of owning your power and moving decisively.
- Best sales strategies: Strong direct offers, pre-sell strategies, and launching with authority.

Reflectors: Selling Through Curated Experiences

- You thrive in sales when you *create* a high-quality, unique *experience* for potential clients.
- Your strength lies in reflecting back what your clients truly need and curating the right solutions.
- If selling feels overwhelming, you may be rushing the decision-making process instead of allowing time for clarity.
- Best sales strategies: Community-based sales, storytelling, and slow-build conversions.

How Your Human Design Environment Influences Your Sales Process

Your Human Design environment is where you feel most comfortable and confident energetically, and this extends to how you approach sales conversations. When you align your sales setting and style with your environment, your confidence and authenticity naturally increase.

Markets: Selling Through Visibility and Opportunity

- You attract clients when you position yourself as an authority in an active space.
- Best approach: Being highly visible and strategic in how you position and price your offers.
- Sales settings: Master classes, networking groups, public-facing platforms, and collaborations.

Caves: Selling in a Safe, Selective Way

- You need to feel secure and in control of your sales environment.
- Best approach: One-on-one, intentional, and intimate sales experiences where you can control the flow.
- Sales settings: Private sales calls, email marketing, and high-ticket, curated offers for select clients.

Shores: Selling in the Right Place at the Right Time

- Your sales energy works best when you create the right environment rather than forcing conversations.
- Best approach: Being strategic about where and how you sell, allowing the right people to come to you.
- Sales settings: Online platforms, networking spaces, social media, or places where people naturally gather.

Kitchens: Selling Through Warmth and Connection

- You thrive in an informal, cozy, conversational approach to sales.
- Best approach: Making offers through community building, nurturing relationships, and having ongoing conversations.
- Sales settings: Live video, casual voice messages in DMs, intimate group settings, and warm audience engagement.

Valleys: Selling Through Community and Conversation

- You thrive in engaged dialogue and direct conversation with your audience.
- Best approach: Sales should feel interactive, conversational, and relationship driven.
- Sales settings: Group coaching, Q&A sessions, community-based sales experiences, and ongoing engagement.

Mountains: Selling from a Higher Perspective

- You thrive when you have space to see the bigger picture rather than being caught in the weeds.

- Best approach: Selling through thought leadership, big-picture strategy, and authority-building content.
- Sales settings: Virtual presentations, podcasting, or recorded content that allows you to share your expertise from a place of wisdom.

Selling Strategies for Each Human Design Profile

Your Human Design Profile plays a crucial role in how you naturally express yourself, build relationships, and engage with potential clients. It shapes the way you connect, communicate, and sell. When you align your sales strategy with your Profile, selling becomes an organic part of your business rather than a forced or uncomfortable task. Below, we'll explore the most aligned selling strategies for each of the twelve Human Design Profiles.

Profile 1/3 – The Investigator/Martyr
Selling Strengths

- Deep knowledge and credibility
- Ability to provide well-researched, grounded explanations
- Natural curiosity that helps uncover client needs

Aligned Selling Strategies

- Lead with education-based content (courses, master classes, in-depth sales pages).
- Offer detailed case studies and research to establish credibility.
- Emphasize trial-and-error wisdom, share real-world experiences and learnings.
- Engage in one-on-one sales conversations where you can investigate and tailor solutions.

Profile 1/4 – The Investigator/Opportunist
Selling Strengths

- Strong foundation of expertise
- Ability to build trust through personal connections
- A powerful network that naturally brings referrals

Aligned Selling Strategies

- Focus on building deep relationships and referral-based marketing.
- Create content that establishes authority (whitepapers, webinars, workshops).
- Leverage warm, personal conversations (DMs, high-touch engagement).
- Use your network, let trusted relationships amplify your sales process.

Profile 2/4 – The Hermit/Opportunist

Selling Strengths

- Magnetism when letting people watch them do what they love
- Authentic, effortless influence within their community
- A balance between needing alone time and thriving in relationships

Aligned Selling Strategies

- Sell through authentic visibility, let people see you in your natural element (behind-the-scenes content, live Q&As).
- Rely on organic word-of-mouth and referrals.
- Avoid aggressive selling; let your natural energy attract the right people.
- Work with small, engaged communities that value your unique skills.

Profile 2/5 – The Hermit/Heretic

Selling Strengths

- Naturally influential and can inspire confidence in others
- Drawn to mastery and depth, making them sought-after experts
- Can deliver practical, bold solutions that others trust

Aligned Selling Strategies

- Lead with strong, bold messaging that positions you as a solution provider.
- Emphasize practical applications and tangible results in your sales process.
- Use speaking engagements, guest interviews, or master classes to draw people in.
- Honor your need for alone time, automate parts of your sales process.

Profile 3/5 – The Martyr/Heretic

Selling Strengths

- Natural ability to learn through experience and share insights
- Strong problem-solving skills that help clients trust them
- A bold, practical presence that influences decision-making

Aligned Selling Strategies

- Sell through real-life mini experiences of what you do at a larger scale.
- Highlight your ability to solve problems quickly and practically.
- Use video content, case studies, and live coaching demos to showcase expertise.
- Make your offers direct and solution oriented.

Profile 3/6 – The Martyr/Role Model

Selling Strengths

- Wisdom gained through real-world experiences
- A natural guide for others who are on a similar journey
- An innate ability to inspire trust and confidence

Aligned Selling Strategies

- Sell through authentic storytelling, share what's worked and what hasn't.

- Offer long-term mentorship programs where people can learn from your experiences.
- Position yourself as a trustworthy guide, rather than just an expert.
- Use a soft, conversational sales approach rather than high-pressure tactics.

Profile 4/1 – The Opportunist/Investigator
Selling Strengths

- Strong personal network and natural ability to influence others
- A grounded approach that combines relationships and expertise
- Ability to attract aligned clients through community connections

Aligned Selling Strategies

- Prioritize relationship-based selling (referrals, collaborations, word-of-mouth).
- Create structured offers that feel solid and well-researched.
- Leverage in-person events or community platforms to nurture sales.
- Establish a reputation as a reliable source of knowledge in your field.

Profile 4/6 – The Opportunist/Role Model
Selling Strengths

- Magnetic presence, people are drawn to their authenticity
- A natural leader who gains trust through experience and relationships
- Ability to guide others with wisdom

Aligned Selling Strategies

- Focus on community engagement and long-term relationships.

- Build a strong personal brand; your presence sells as much as your offer.
- Sell through content that reflects your values, lifestyle, and leadership.
- Let people in your community come to you; don't force sales conversations.

Profile 5/1 – The Heretic/Investigator

Selling Strengths

- Ability to deliver practical, game-changing solutions
- Strong authority and leadership presence
- Can easily diagnose what people need and offer solutions

Aligned Selling Strategies

- Position yourself as a trusted guide and problem-solver.
- Use structured launches, high-value content, and authority-building strategies.
- Sell through confident messaging; people trust you when you stand firm.
- Educate through well-researched, solution-driven sales content.

Profile 5/2 – The Heretic/Hermit

Selling Strengths

- Charismatic presence that naturally draws people in
- Strong leadership abilities, even when working behind the scenes
- Ability to see the big picture and provide strategic solutions

Aligned Selling Strategies

- Sell through a mix of visible leadership and deep, intentional work.
- Make sure you have alone time; you don't need to be constantly selling.
- Use impactful sales pages, strategic launches, and confident positioning.

- Work with clients who recognize your value and trust your solutions.

Profile 6/2 – The Role Model/Hermit

Selling Strengths

- A natural mentor and leader
- Gains deep wisdom from personal experiences
- Authentic, grounded, and naturally influential

Aligned Selling Strategies

- Focus on mentorship-based sales, long-term programs, and deep trust-building.
- Sell through stories and real-life examples; show, don't just tell.
- Use nurturing, high-touch sales methods rather than quick conversions.
- Leverage authority-building content (podcasts, books, speaking engagements).

Profile 6/3 – The Role Model/Experimenter

Selling Strengths

- Deep, lived wisdom from real experiences
- A natural innovator and guide
- Ability to relate to others through trial-and-error learning

Aligned Selling Strategies

- Sell through authentic storytelling and personal growth insights.
- Create high-ticket, wisdom-driven offers (masterminds, mentorships).
- Focus on relationship-building and trust-based sales strategies.
- Offer custom, experiential, or transformational sales experiences.

Practical Application Exercise: Reflection Questions

Reflection is key to refining your sales strategy and ensuring alignment with your energy, business goals, and Human Design. Take time to answer these questions honestly, as they will provide clarity on what's working, what's not, and where adjustments need to be made.

Reflection Questions

1. Where specifically are you selling your offers?
   - Are you primarily selling through sales calls, social media, webinars, email marketing, or direct conversations?
   - Which platforms or methods feel natural and effective to you?

2. How frequently are you making offers?
   - Do you have a consistent rhythm for selling, or is it sporadic?
   - Are you only selling during launches, or do you also have evergreen offers?

3. Are the places you are making offers converting to sales?
   - Which sales methods are leading to actual client sign-ups and purchases?
   - Are certain platforms, conversations, or approaches converting better than others?

4. Does your current sales process feel aligned with your Human Design energy?
   - Are you selling in a way that feels authentic and energizing?
   - If sales feel draining, what needs to shift?

5. What objections do you commonly hear from potential clients?
   - Are there patterns in why people hesitate to buy?
   - How can you refine your messaging, positioning, or offer structure to address these?

6. How clear is your sales messaging?

- Can potential clients easily understand what you offer, how it helps, and how to take action?
- Do you need to refine your sales page, pitch, or call to action?

7. Are you creating enough opportunities for people to say yes?

- How often are you giving your audience a clear invitation to work with you?
- Do you need to increase visibility, outreach, or nurturing efforts?

8. What sales strategies feel best to you?

- Do you enjoy direct sales calls, interactive workshops, email marketing, or passive sales funnels?
- How can you do more of what feels natural and effective?

By answering these questions, you'll gain clarity on where to fine-tune your sales approach, increase visibility, and remove friction in your sales process.

Common Mistakes to Avoid

Even the most seasoned entrepreneurs can fall into common sales pitfalls. Being aware of these mistakes can help you course-correct quickly and sell in a way that feels natural and aligned.

- **Not Selling Frequently Enough**
  One of the biggest reasons entrepreneurs struggle with sales is simply not selling enough. Many business owners feel uncomfortable promoting their offers and assume that if they mention it once, people will remember. The reality? People need multiple touchpoints before making a decision. Fix this by making selling a regular and intentional part of your content strategy. Use a mix of direct invitations, nurturing content, and follow-ups to create a flow that feels natural.

- **Not Having a Sales Process (a.k.a. Winging It)**

Relying on spontaneous, unstructured selling can lead to inconsistent results. If you don't have a clear process for bringing in leads, nurturing them, and closing sales, your business will struggle to maintain predictable revenue. Document your sales process, know how leads find you, how you nurture them, and what your conversion strategy is. Set up automations, follow-up sequences, or structured sales cycles that create consistency. Review and refine your sales system every quarter to optimize what's working.

- **Forcing Yourself to Sell in a Way That Feels Inauthentic**
  Many entrepreneurs try to follow traditional, high-pressure sales tactics that don't align with their energy. This often leads to burnout, misalignment, and discomfort around selling.

Align your sales strategy with your Human Design Type, strengths, and natural communication style. Choose sales methods that feel energizing and sustainable. Focus on relationship-based selling rather than aggressive tactics.

Remember, selling is not about convincing people to buy, it's about clear and aligned communication that effectively shows people your business is the right fit for them. When you structure your sales process in a way that feels natural to you and deeply supportive of your ideal clients, selling becomes a seamless, confident, and natural part of your business.

CHAPTER 11

ORGANIZATIONAL AND OPERATIONAL STRUCTURE

Understanding Intentional Business Structure

By this point I hope you see how a business's success is determined by so many components, including having a clear vision, understanding your niche, creating aligned offers, and so much more. But a huge key that is often an afterthought is the infrastructure that allows a business to function effectively and sustainably. This chapter focuses on the who, what, and how behind fulfilling your business's mission and delivering your unique value proposition.

When we talk about the structure of your business, we are referring to the combination of people, software, systems, and processes that ensure everything runs smoothly. Whether you're a solopreneur, working with a small team, or scaling up, defining your operational framework is crucial.

One of the biggest mistakes entrepreneurs make is trying to do too much on their own or waiting too long to hire help. Many entrepreneurs have a hard time delegating tasks because they are concerned about paying for the help, or perhaps believe they are the only ones who can do the activity properly. For example, I coached a healer who wanted to scale beyond her one-to-one work, but she feared that shifting into a course or group model would not be as effective as the one-to-one work. She was also doing all the backend tech activities, front-end marketing and sales, and doing her own bookkeeping. Eventually she realized that slowing down enough to hire support for the non-client work would free up her time to take on more clients. This also allowed her to have space in her calendar to obtain additional training in new healing modalities, which caused her to raise her prices as well.

Still, there's a common belief for many entrepreneurs that if you're not "doing it all," you're somehow not working hard enough or not maximizing profits. However, the reality is that running a business efficiently requires delegation, automation, and strategic support. Your business model may even require a more complex or intricate structure based on the type of business you are building, speed at which you want to grow, or skills needed to fulfill your mission and services.

Take my business for example. When I founded the Spiritual Business Incubator, my vision was to create a company that didn't just serve at a surface level but also deeply supported spiritual entrepreneurs to start, evolve, or scale their mission-driven businesses with clarity, confidence, and alignment. At the heart of this vision is a consciously designed organizational structure, one that allows me to fully embody my zone of genius as the visionary and leader of the aligned business movement.

From the beginning, I knew the business vision was not meant to rely solely on me to operate and deliver its services. I made this intentional decision for so many reasons, including the fact that the impact I wanted to make required structure to support clients at the high level I desired, that I am a 5/2 Sacral Generator and knew that I wanted to balance my personal visibility with reflective alone time, and the fact that I am a wife and mama who wants to be present in my family's lives. That's why I have been strategically building a sustainable and scalable infrastructure that brings in *subject matter experts* and *skilled team members* to manage backend operations, elevate client support, and enhance the overall experience of the Spiritual Business Incubator's programs.

The operational structure is intentionally designed so I can stay focused on moving the business forward through my zone of genius, then investing in people and systems that will support growing my business vision at the speed I desire.

Organizational structure is the part of business that isn't talked about enough. Many entrepreneurs put all their focus on attracting clients, selling offers, and delivering services, but without a solid operational structure, even the best businesses can become unsustainable.

As you reflect on your business, consider these key questions:

- How is your business currently delivering its products or services?
- Are you relying solely on yourself, or do you have support (team members, software, or systems)?
- What bottlenecks exist in your processes?
- Are you building with long-term vision in mind or simply reacting to immediate needs?

Your business structure needs to support not just your current operations but also the future growth you envision. This means ensuring that you are not only serving your clients effectively today but also creating a business model that can scale with ease and alignment.

The Purpose Behind Organizational and Operational Structure

Clarity around your organizational and operational structure helps you move beyond working reactively and step into intentional growth. Understanding how your business operates at a foundational level ensures that:

- **You identify whether people or systems are doing the work.**
  - Some tasks require human touch (coaching, consulting, client engagement), while others can be

streamlined through automation, templates, or AI-powered tools.

- If everything is dependent on you, your business isn't truly sustainable. Defining which aspects need human attention and which need to be systems and can be automated creates efficiency and ease.

- **You distinguish between recurring activities versus one-time tasks.**
    - Some tasks, like client onboarding, marketing content, and email communication, happen on a recurring basis and need efficient workflows.

    - Other tasks, like launching a new program or creating a website, are one-time projects but require structured planning to ensure completion.

    - Knowing the difference allows you to optimize your time, delegate effectively, and prevent burnout.

- **Your clients are well-served.**
    - A strong business structure isn't just about making your life easier, it's about creating a seamless, high-quality experience for your clients.

    - Whether they are booking services, receiving deliverables, or interacting with your brand, every touchpoint should feel intentional and aligned with your mission.

- **Your business supports the life you desire.**
    - Your business should not feel like a constant uphill battle; it should be a vehicle for freedom, abundance, and flow.

    - A well-organized structure ensures you're not constantly in reaction mode but instead making strategic, aligned decisions that allow you to thrive both professionally and personally.

- **You stay in your zone of genius and align with your Human Design.**
    - Your Human Design provides powerful insights into how you work best. Are you a visionary who thrives on strategy and big-picture thinking? Or are you energized by hands-on creation and collaboration?

    - Knowing your strengths and designing your business accordingly allows you to stay in alignment rather than forcing yourself into roles that drain you.

    - Hiring, delegating, or automating should be approached from a place of energetic alignment so you can focus on what truly lights you up.

Your business structure is the invisible foundation that holds everything together. By taking a conscious and intentional approach to your people, systems, processes, and long-term vision, you create a business that is scalable, sustainable, and deeply aligned with your mission.

The goal is not just to manage your business but to design it in a way that supports both your clients' success and your own well-being. The more clarity you have around who is responsible for what, how tasks get completed, and which systems support your growth, the more confidently you can step into your role as the visionary and leader of your business.

Different Types of Business Structures and Their Evolution

Business structures range from simple to complex, and understanding where you are in this evolution is key to making intentional choices. There is no one-size-fits-all approach, as the ideal structure depends on your business goals, available resources, and long-term vision.

Simple Versus Complex Business Structures

Many entrepreneurs start with a simple structure, often as solopreneurs handling every aspect of their business. While this allows for complete control and minimal financial overhead, it also creates potential burnout and limits scalability. Over time, businesses evolve to incorporate more sophisticated structures involving teams, systems, and automation.

A **simple structure** may consist of:

- A single entrepreneur managing all operations
- Basic tools and software for scheduling, invoicing, and communication
- Minimal delegation, with most tasks handled manually

A **complex structure** may include the following:

- Multiple team members (contractors, employees, or strategic partners)
- Defined departments or functional areas (marketing, sales, operations, fulfillment)
- Advanced systems and automation to streamline workflows

The Natural Evolution of Business Structures

As businesses grow, their structures naturally shift based on increased demand, new opportunities, and evolving priorities. Entrepreneurs often move through several stages:

- **Solopreneur Stage:** Handling everything alone, learning through experience
- **Outsourcing Stage:** Bringing in help (virtual assistants, independent contractors) to relieve workload
- **Team Building Stage:** Hiring permanent staff, establishing processes and leadership roles
- **Scalability Stage:** Expanding operations, refining systems, and optimizing efficiency

We will dive more into these in an upcoming section, but what matters most is that you start to realize that certain goals require certain structures. Growth doesn't have to mean building a massive corporation; it means being intentional about how the business operates and evolves.

Starting Small and Expanding

"Small" is relative. What feels manageable to one entrepreneur may feel overwhelming to another. Consider these two different models:

- **A solo massage therapist running a home-based practice.** This entrepreneur may handle all tasks, from client scheduling to bookkeeping, but could later bring in administrative help or use software to streamline operations.
- **A wellness center with multiple practitioners.** This entrepreneur may start by offering services personally but later step into a CEO role, hiring staff to expand offerings and delegate responsibilities.

The most important thing is being intentional with what you ultimately want to create, then creating a plan to grow strategically based on your vision, resources, and capacity.

Key Considerations for Choosing the Right Business Structure

When determining the best structure for your business, consider the following:

- **Mission and Impact:** How expansive is your vision? Do you want a small, intimate practice, or do you see your business growing into a large-scale enterprise? Your structure should support your ability to fulfill your mission.
- **Timeline:** Are you looking for rapid growth, or do you prefer a steady, organic expansion? The speed at which you want to achieve your goals influences how many resources (people, systems, capital) you need to allocate.
- **Your Skills Versus Business Needs:** Where do you thrive? Which tasks energize you and which drain you? Your business structure should be designed to allow you to stay in your zone of genius while delegating or automating areas that aren't your strengths.

- **Resources:** Every business operates within the constraints of time, energy, and money. Consider how much of each you have available and where you want to invest strategically to support sustainable growth.

Your business structure should be an extension of your vision and values, built to support both your clients and your personal well-being. There is no right or wrong way, only what aligns with your goals and the lifestyle you want to create.

By approaching business structure with intentionality and flexibility, you set yourself up for long-term success, whether you remain a solopreneur or build a large-scale company. The next section will guide you through mapping out your organizational structure and operational workflows, helping you refine your approach and establish a strong foundation for sustainable growth.

Business Elements to Consider When Designing Your Structure

In Which Stage of Business Are You?

The stage of business you are in significantly impacts the type of organizational and operational structure that best supports your growth. Without recognizing where you currently stand, you risk either understructuring your business and becoming overwhelmed or over-structuring too early, leading to unnecessary complexity and expenses. Each stage comes with its own challenges, priorities, and needs, making it essential to align your business framework accordingly.

1. **Solopreneur Stage:** At this stage, you handle every aspect of the business, from marketing to service delivery and admin tasks. Your primary goal is efficiency, and your structure should include basic tools, automation, and streamlined workflows to minimize burnout.

2. **Outsourcing Stage:** As your workload increases, you recognize the need to delegate. The focus shifts to identifying what can be outsourced, such as administrative support, content creation, or client onboarding. Setting up standard

operating procedures (SOPs) and automated systems becomes a priority to maintain consistency.

3. **Team Building Stage:** You begin hiring dedicated team members or contractors for specific roles. Organizational structure becomes crucial to define clear responsibilities, communication channels, and performance expectations. At this stage, investing in project management tools and leadership development ensures smooth operations.

4. **Scaling Stage:** Your focus moves from daily execution to high-level strategy, leadership, and scaling efforts. A well-established operational structure, including documented workflows, financial management, and advanced automation is essential to sustain business growth while maintaining efficiency.

Recognizing your stage enables you to implement the right level of organization, ensuring that your business remains functional, scalable, and aligned with your vision. Understanding what stage your business is in helps clarify your next steps. Are you a solopreneur juggling multiple roles, a growing business starting to outsource, or a scaling enterprise focused on leadership and delegation?

Identifying your stage ensures you make informed decisions about structure and operations.

Solopreneur Stage

At this stage, you are the sole operator responsible for every facet of your business, including client service, marketing, administrative tasks, and financial management. This phase requires immense discipline and organization, as you wear multiple hats daily. The key challenge here is balancing all responsibilities without burning out.

To navigate this stage effectively, solopreneurs must leverage automation, prioritize high-impact tasks, and set clear boundaries. Using digital tools for scheduling, invoicing, email marketing, and task management can significantly reduce workload and streamline operations. Additionally, developing a structured workflow for client onboarding, service delivery, and follow-up can improve efficiency and ensure a seamless customer experience.

While the solopreneur stage offers complete control over decision-making and flexibility, it can also be isolating and overwhelming. Recognizing the limitations of this stage is crucial. Eventually, to scale and sustain growth, solopreneurs need to consider delegation, outsourcing, or systematization. The goal is to build a strong operational foundation that allows for expansion while maintaining quality and efficiency.

Outsourcing Stage

As your workload increases, you recognize the need to delegate non-essential or time-consuming tasks. This stage is a turning point where entrepreneurs shift from doing everything themselves to leveraging external support. The focus here is on identifying tasks that can be outsourced to freelancers, virtual assistants, or automation tools, allowing you to concentrate on higher-value activities that align with your expertise and business growth.

Key considerations in this stage:

- **Identifying what to outsource:** Tasks such as administrative work, customer support, bookkeeping, and content creation are common first steps.
- **Finding the right support:** Hiring reliable contractors or virtual assistants requires clear job descriptions, structured onboarding, and effective communication.
- **Building systems for consistency:** Documenting standard operating procedures ensures that outsourced tasks maintain the same quality and efficiency as if you were handling them yourself.
- **Leveraging automation:** Implementing tools for email marketing, client onboarding, invoicing, and customer service can significantly streamline operations and reduce manual effort.

This stage is about reclaiming your time, preventing burnout, and preparing your business for scalability. When outsourcing is done strategically, it sets the foundation for smooth business growth, paving the way for hiring dedicated team members in the next stage.

Team Building Stage

At this stage, you transition from outsourcing individual tasks to assembling a team of dedicated employees or long-term contractors. This marks a shift in business structure from solo execution to leadership and management. The primary focus is on hiring strategically, defining clear roles, and ensuring effective collaboration.

Key elements of the team-building stage:

- **Recruiting the Right People:** Hiring employees or contractors who align with your business values, mission, and work ethic is essential. Consider factors such as skills, experience, and cultural fit when bringing people into your business.
- **Defining Workflows and Responsibilities:** Creating clear job descriptions and structured workflows helps ensure accountability and efficiency. This involves documenting standard operating procedures for each role, setting key performance indicators, and establishing reporting structures.
- **Developing Leadership Skills:** As a business owner, your role shifts from doing to leading. Investing in leadership development, communication skills, and team management ensures you can effectively guide your growing team.
- **Implementing Collaboration Tools:** Effective teamwork relies on seamless communication and task management. Leveraging project management tools, shared calendars, and team communication platforms (such as Slack, Trello, or Asana) enhances efficiency and productivity.
- **Building a Strong Company Culture:** A positive work environment fosters employee satisfaction and retention. Encouraging open communication, recognizing achievements, and creating opportunities for professional growth contribute to a motivated team.

The team-building stage is about expanding your capacity and creating a self-sustaining operation where responsibilities are distributed, allowing the business to grow beyond the limitations of a single individual. With the right people, systems, and leadership in place, you establish a strong foundation for scaling to the next level.

Scaling Stage

At this stage, your focus shifts from the day-to-day operations to high-level strategy, leadership, and optimizing efficiency across teams. Your primary goal is to refine the structure of your business so that it can operate smoothly and grow sustainably without requiring your constant involvement.

Key elements of the scaling stage:

- **Optimizing Systems and Processes:** By refining and automating workflows, you ensure that operations run seamlessly. This may include integrating advanced customer relationship management (CRM) systems, streamlining internal communications, and improving client management systems.
- **Building Strong Leadership:** At this point, your leadership team becomes critical. You may appoint department heads or managers who take on operational oversight, allowing you to focus on vision, growth, and business expansion.
- **Developing Scalable Revenue Streams:** Expanding product lines, creating licensing opportunities, launching franchises, or increasing market penetration all contribute to scaling without solely relying on direct client work.
- **Financial and Resource Management:** Scaling requires careful financial planning to ensure cash flow stability and strategic reinvestments. This might include securing funding, optimizing pricing structures, or expanding your service capacity.
- **Expanding Your Brand Presence:** Strengthening your marketing and sales funnels to reach a wider audience is essential. This could involve digital marketing expansion, partnerships, or international business opportunities.
- **Maintaining Company Culture and Employee Engagement:** As your team grows, fostering a strong culture and

ensuring alignment with your company's values becomes increasingly important.

This stage is about sustainability, optimization, and expansion. The right combination of leadership, technology, and strategic investments ensures that your business can continue growing while maintaining efficiency and profitability.

What Role Do You Want to Play?

Have you ever actually thought about this? Many of the clients I work with started their businesses because they want to help people by sharing their gifts through the unique way they teach, heal, serve, etc. They quickly learn that entrepreneurship is so much more complex and that there are many roles required to make a business successful. Determining the business role that you want to play within your business is crucial for long-term sustainability, fulfillment, and efficiency. Your business needs all the components that I teach you about in this book, and you—as the business owner—are responsible for making sure each one is aligned to your mission and you as the leader. As your business grows, your responsibilities and involvement will evolve, and it's important to proactively define where your time and energy are best spent at each stage of business growth. This clarity allows you to align your work with your strengths, ensure strategic decision-making, and delegate appropriately.

Making the Shift to Your Ideal Role

Once you have clarity on your ideal role, the next step is to transition intentionally. This might involve the following:

- Delegating or outsourcing tasks that fall outside of your zone of genius
- Hiring key team members who can manage areas you no longer want to oversee directly
- Investing in leadership development to step into a CEO mindset
- Implementing automation and systems to streamline business operations

By aligning your business structure with your natural strengths and preferred working style, you create a business that supports not only your financial goals but also your personal fulfillment and long-term success. Defining your desired role in your business is crucial for long-term sustainability and fulfillment.

Who or What Completes Business Activities?

Every business function requires a clear assignment of responsibility, whether to a person or a system. Without clarity on who or what is handling essential activities, inefficiencies and bottlenecks can arise, leading to decreased productivity and inconsistent client experiences.

People Versus Systems: Finding the Right Balance in Business Operations

Every business, no matter the size, operates through a combination of human effort and automated systems. Understanding the balance between people-driven tasks and system-driven automation is critical for scalability, efficiency, and sustainability. Some aspects of a business require direct human involvement, such as client interactions, strategic decision-making, and creative development. Others can be streamlined through automation, reducing manual effort and allowing the business to run more smoothly. Striking the right balance means knowing where to prioritize human energy and where to let systems handle the work.

The Role of People: Human-Centered Aspects of Business

At its core, business is about people, relationships, leadership, and expertise. Human touch is necessary for tasks that require creativity, emotional intelligence, and critical thinking. These roles often include the following:

- **Client Interaction and Service:** Personalized communication, coaching, consulting, and customer support require empathy, adaptability, and active listening—qualities that automation can't replicate.

- **Leadership and Vision:** Business strategy, innovation, and decision-making rely on intuitive leadership and human experience. A system can process data, but only people can interpret it in the context of vision and purpose.
- **Creative Work and Brand Identity:** Whether it's content creation, graphic design, or storytelling, human creativity is essential for authentic expression and maintaining a brand's unique voice.
- **Sales and Relationship Building:** While automation can help nurture leads, deep conversations and high-touch selling require human connection, especially for high-ticket offers.

The human element is what makes a business relatable, trusted, and dynamic. But relying too heavily on people for every task can lead to burnout, inefficiencies, and limited scalability, which is where systems come in.

The Role of Systems: Automation for Efficiency and Growth

Technology exists to support business operations, reducing the need for manual work in areas that don't require human judgment. Systems create efficiency, consistency, and scalability, allowing entrepreneurs to focus their energy where it truly matters.

Common areas where automation can enhance efficiency:

- **Invoicing and Payments:** Automated billing ensures payments are processed on time without the need for manual follow-ups.
- **Email Marketing and Follow-Ups:** Sequences and autoresponders nurture leads, keeping engagement consistent without requiring daily effort.
- **Scheduling and Appointments:** Tools like Calendly or Acuity handle booking logistics, eliminating back-and-forth communication.
- **Content Distribution:** Social media scheduling platforms automate posting so businesses can maintain visibility without daily manual effort.

- **Data and Reporting:** AI-powered analytics provide insights into business performance, helping entrepreneurs make informed decisions.

When used strategically, systems free up time and mental energy, allowing business owners to focus on big-picture growth and personal fulfillment rather than being stuck in repetitive tasks.

Creating a Business That Works for You

The most successful businesses don't rely solely on people or entirely on automation. Instead, they integrate both in a way that optimizes productivity while maintaining a personal, human touch.

- Where do you need to show up personally to create impact? (Client sessions, sales calls, content creation?)
- Where can you automate without losing authenticity? (Email sequences, payments, backend operations?)

By identifying what requires your energy versus what can be systemized, you create a business that is both aligned and sustainable, one that feels good to run while allowing for scalability and flow.

Key Business Roles and Their Functions

Every business requires a well-defined structure to operate efficiently and sustainably. Understanding the essential roles within your business, whether fulfilled by individuals or automated systems, helps streamline operations and ensure long-term success. Below is a deeper breakdown of each role and its significance in business growth and sustainability.

Client Delivery: The core of your business—ensuring products or services meet and exceed customer expectations.

- **Responsibilities:** Direct engagement with clients, service execution, product fulfillment, maintaining quality standards, gathering client feedback, and ensuring customer satisfaction
- **Who:** You, contractors, or in-house employees dedicated to service delivery

- **Systems and Tools:** Client relationship management software (e.g., HubSpot, Salesforce), scheduling platforms (e.g., Calendly, Acuity), project management tools (e.g., Asana, Trello), and automated client follow-up systems
- **Key Considerations:** Efficient client delivery requires structured workflows to handle onboarding, service implementation, and follow-ups seamlessly.

Marketing and Sales: Attracting, nurturing, and converting leads into paying customers through effective engagement strategies.

- **Responsibilities:** Content creation, email marketing, social media management, advertising, lead nurturing, client acquisition, and sales calls
- **Who:** Marketing managers, copywriters, social media strategists, sales representatives, or agencies
- **Systems and Tools:** Social media scheduling tools (e.g., Buffer, Later), email marketing automation (e.g., Kit, ActiveCampaign), lead capture and nurturing CRM (e.g., Pipedrive, Keap), digital advertising platforms (e.g., Google Ads, Facebook Ads)
- **Key Considerations:** A consistent marketing strategy ensures a predictable revenue stream and brand growth.

Finance and Operations: Managing the financial health and operational efficiency of your business.

- **Responsibilities:** Budgeting, invoicing, financial tracking, tax compliance, payroll processing, operational efficiency, and business sustainability
- **Who:** Accountants, bookkeepers, CFOs, or financial consultants
- **Systems and Tools:** Accounting software (e.g., QuickBooks, FreshBooks), invoicing and payment automation (e.g., Stripe, PayPal), financial planning software (e.g., Xero, Wave), expense tracking tools
- **Key Considerations:** Proper financial management ensures stability, profitability, and the ability to scale strategically.

Leadership and Human Resources (HR): Managing the team, company culture, and strategic direction.

- **Responsibilities:** Talent acquisition, hiring, onboarding, team development, leadership, organizational structure, and business vision.
- **Who:** CEO, HR managers, leadership consultants, or operational managers.
- **Systems and Tools:** HR software (e.g., BambooHR, Gusto), employee engagement tools, project management software for remote teams.
- **Key Considerations:** Strong leadership and HR practices enhance productivity, company culture, and long-term retention of talented employees.

Customer Experience and Support: Ensuring ongoing client satisfaction, troubleshooting, and retention.

- **Responsibilities:** Handling inquiries, providing after-sales support, processing refunds or adjustments, resolving customer concerns, and enhancing the overall user experience
- **Who:** Customer service reps, support teams, community managers, or automated chatbots
- **Systems and Tools:** Helpdesk platforms (e.g., Zendesk, Freshdesk), AI-powered chatbots, ticketing systems, feedback collection tools
- **Key Considerations:** Excellent customer service builds brand loyalty, increases referrals, and improves retention rates.

Business Development and Innovation: Identifying new opportunities for growth, partnerships, and market expansion.

- **Responsibilities:** Researching industry trends, forging partnerships, business model innovation, revenue diversification, and product or service expansion
- **Who:** Business owner, strategic consultants, advisory boards, or industry analysts
- **Systems and Tools:** Market research platforms, networking tools, strategic planning software

- **Key Considerations:** Continuously evolving and adapting ensures long-term business resilience and growth.

Implementing These Roles Effectively

Once you have identified the key roles within your business, the next step is to ensure they are implemented effectively to create a structured, scalable, and sustainable operation. Implementation involves careful planning, delegation, documentation, and systematization to optimize efficiency and prevent bottlenecks.

Role Assignment and Responsibility Clarity

Every role in your business should have clearly defined responsibilities to avoid confusion and ensure accountability. This includes the following:

- Assigning ownership of each function (e.g., who handles marketing, client service, financial management)
- Clarifying expectations, deliverables, and performance metrics for each role
- Ensuring that employees, contractors, or systems executing these roles have the right tools and training to succeed

By creating detailed role descriptions and defining workflows, you ensure that each component of the business functions efficiently, regardless of who is executing the tasks.

Standard Operating Procedures (SOPs) and Workflow Documentation

One of the most critical steps in implementing roles effectively is creating documented workflows. SOPs provide a roadmap for executing tasks efficiently and consistently, reducing errors, and making delegation easier.

- **Why SOPs Matter**
  - Ensures consistency in task execution across different team members

- Provides clear guidelines to reduce the learning curve for new hires
- Increases efficiency by eliminating guesswork and confusion
- Allows for easier troubleshooting and performance assessment

- **What to Include in SOPs**
  - Step-by-step instructions for executing key tasks
  - Expected timelines and deadlines for completion
  - Tools and resources required for the task
  - Common troubleshooting steps and solutions
  - Key contacts for escalation

Every repeatable process in your business, from client onboarding to content creation and financial tracking, should have an SOP in place.

Performance Metrics and Key Performance Indicators (KPIs)

For each role, establish measurable key performance indicators (KPIs) to track performance and effectiveness. These metrics provide insight into what is working well and what needs improvement.

Examples of KPIs by role

- **Client Delivery:** Client retention rates, satisfaction scores, project completion time
- **Marketing and Sales:** Lead conversion rates, cost per lead, email open rates
- **Finance and Operations:** Revenue growth, profit margins, expense ratios
- **Customer Experience and Support:** Response time, resolution rate, customer reviews

By tracking these metrics, you can make data-driven decisions to refine operations, optimize processes, and improve overall business performance. Without metrics, your emotions may take the reins of your business and that may result in decisions that waste time, energy, and money on things not aligned with the highest potential of your business mission.

Automation Versus Delegation

A well-implemented business structure utilizes both automation and human delegation to maximize efficiency. Knowing what tasks can be automated versus those that require a human touch allows you to scale effectively without overburdening yourself or your team.

Tasks Suitable for Automation

- Email marketing campaigns and follow-ups
- Appointment scheduling and reminders
- Invoice generation and financial reporting
- Social media post scheduling

Tasks Best Delegated to People

- Sales calls and relationship-building
- Client support and high-touch customer service
- Leadership and strategic decision-making
- Creative content creation and branding

By implementing automation where appropriate, you free up time for higher-value activities that require creativity and human insight.

Continuous Improvement and Scalability Planning

Business structures are not static; they evolve as your company grows. Regularly reviewing and refining your operational framework ensures continued efficiency and scalability.

- Conduct quarterly or annual operational reviews to assess what is working and what needs improvement.
- Seek feedback from employees, contractors, or clients to optimize processes.
- Invest in training and professional development for your team to enhance their skill sets and performance.

- Stay updated with emerging tools and technologies that can further streamline business operations.

By implementing these strategies, businesses can create an efficient, well-structured system that supports growth while maintaining high-quality service and operational consistency. The ultimate goal is to build a business that runs smoothly without constant hands-on involvement, allowing for greater flexibility, profitability, and long-term sustainability.

Practical Application Exercise: Reflection Questions to Identify Your Ideal Role

Defining Your Ideal Role

Reflecting on your role in the business is the first step toward creating an aligned and sustainable structure. Consider these key questions:

- What aspects of your business energize and excite you?
- Where do you add the most value to the business?
- What responsibilities feel draining or outside your expertise?
- How do you envision your ideal day-to-day work experience?
- Are you operating in alignment with your Human Design or zone of genius?

Clarity on these questions allows you to structure your business in a way that aligns with your natural strengths and avoids burnout.

Common Mistakes to Avoid

Many entrepreneurs unknowingly create unnecessary roadblocks that hinder their business growth and sustainability. Here are some common mistakes to watch out for:

- Not being clear on the role that is right for you and instead trying to do things like other people. Each entrepreneur's strengths and working style are different. Building a business that aligns with your personal energy and skills will lead to better results than copying someone else's approach.

- Doing everything yourself for too long. Holding onto every task stifles growth and limits your ability to scale. Delegation and systematization are essential for freeing up time and focusing on high-value activities.
- Thinking you have to reach a certain point/revenue in order to hire support. Many entrepreneurs delay hiring or outsourcing because they believe they need to earn a certain amount first. However, bringing in support early can accelerate business growth by freeing up your time for higher-value tasks.
- Not being clear if you personally need to gain a skill or perspective or if you need to hire someone to do this for you. There are times when investing in coaching, courses, or training is the best approach to expand your skills and other times when hiring a specialist is the better move. Knowing when to upskill yourself versus outsourcing a function is key to efficient business growth.

By avoiding these common mistakes and being intentional with your business structure, you set yourself up for long-term success with clarity, efficiency, and ease.

CHAPTER 12

BUSINESS BUILDING RESOURCES AND FINANCIAL PLAN

What Are Business Building Resources?

Businesses require critical resources to build them in the form of time, energy, and money. The process of identifying the specific resources necessary to create and sustain the business you have designed is a fundamental part of ensuring you can actually achieve your desired vision. The process of acquiring these looks different from person to person and business to business. Some people choose to use a lot of their own time because they want to use their money for something else. Others use money to hire people to do the work required to build the business. These are some of the choices you get to make as an entrepreneur along with choosing the timing and strategy for utilizing these resources effectively.

This process will look different depending on what stage of business you are in. The key is to make conscious decisions about resource allocation and set boundaries around how and when you trade these resources. As your business evolves, so should your approach to resource management.

The Importance of Resources in Business

One of the most overlooked aspects of business building is the necessity of resources. In the early stage of business, so many entrepreneurs are trying to do everything themselves—even if they have no idea what they are doing or don't like what they are doing. This is a fast road to burnout and painfully slow business growth. Then as your business is ready to evolve or scale, if you don't have the necessary resources to make that happen, it could lead to no momentum or negative client experiences. Without a solid understanding of what is required to build and sustain a business, entrepreneurs often find themselves unnecessarily struggling. I have thought a lot about why this happens.

The Three Core Resources for Building a Business

At its most fundamental level, every business is built and sustained through three key resources: time, energy, and money. These resources are deeply interconnected, and the way you allocate them determines your ability to grow, scale, and maintain an aligned, sustainable business. Entrepreneurs often find themselves balancing these resources, making strategic decisions about where to invest more heavily depending on their current business stage, goals, and personal capacity. While in some circles, money is often considered a form of energy, for the purpose of building a tangible, 3D business, we will treat money as a separate and distinct resource.

Time: The Nonrenewable Resource

Time is one of the most valuable yet nonrenewable resources in business. Every entrepreneur has the same twenty-four hours in a day, but how that time is allocated directly impacts business success and sustainability.

How Time Impacts Business Growth

- The amount of time spent on strategy, execution, and client work affects overall business momentum.

- Entrepreneurs in early stages often invest more time to compensate for a lower budget, handling tasks themselves instead of outsourcing.
- As a business scales, time must be leveraged strategically, moving from hands-on work to leadership, delegation, and automation.

Key Questions to Evaluate Time Investment

- Where is my time best spent for the highest return?
- What tasks am I doing that could be delegated or automated?
- Am I spending too much time in busy work instead of revenue-generating activities?

The key is to protect your time, prioritizing high-impact activities while eliminating distractions, inefficiencies, and unnecessary tasks.

Energy: The Fuel for Sustainable Success

Energy is often overlooked in traditional business models, but for visionary entrepreneurs, it is one of the most critical resources. Unlike time and money, energy is not just about how much you have, it's about how well you manage, replenish, and align it with your natural flow.

How Energy Impacts Business Success

- Your mental, emotional, and physical state influences productivity, creativity, and decision-making.
- Business activities that feel energizing and fulfilling are more sustainable than those that lead to burnout.
- Entrepreneurs must learn to recognize where their energy thrives and structure their work accordingly.

Key Questions to Evaluate Energy Investment

- Do my daily tasks feel aligned with my strengths and Human Design?
- Where do I feel energized versus drained in my business?
- Am I giving myself enough time for rest, creativity, and renewal?

Aligning strategy with energetic sustainability ensures long-term success without burnout, creating a business that fuels you rather than depletes you.

Money: The Resource That Creates Leverage

Money is a powerful resource that provides opportunities, scalability, and financial stability. While time and energy are more intangible, money allows business owners to buy back time, optimize systems, and create more ease in business growth.

How Money Impacts Business Growth

- In the early stages, entrepreneurs may need to reinvest earnings to fund tools, mentorship, or marketing.
- Scaling requires financial investment in hiring, automation, and business growth strategies.
- Understanding how to generate, manage, and invest money wisely is essential for sustainability.

Key Questions to Evaluate Money Investment

- Am I investing in the right areas to grow my business sustainably?
- Where can I spend money to save time or increase efficiency?
- Do I have a financial plan that aligns with my business goals?

Money provides leverage, but clarity around financial decisions ensures that investments lead to growth rather than unnecessary expenses.

The Balance Between Time, Energy, and Money

At different stages of business, the balance between these three resources shifts.

- In the beginning, entrepreneurs often invest more time and energy while their finances are limited.
- As the business grows, money becomes a key leverage point, allowing for outsourcing, automation, and systemization.
- For long-term sustainability, entrepreneurs must continually optimize their use of time, energy, and money to maintain growth without exhaustion.

By consciously managing these three core resources, you can build a business that not only thrives financially but also aligns with your personal well-being and long-term vision.

The Resource Exchange

Every decision you make in business involves an exchange of one or more of these resources:

- You may trade *time* to gain more *money* by handling tasks yourself rather than outsourcing.
- You may invest *money* to save *time and energy* by hiring support or automating processes.
- You may preserve *energy* by setting boundaries, ensuring you operate in alignment with your natural flow rather than depleting yourself.

Understanding this exchange is crucial for making intentional, aligned decisions about how to grow and sustain your business. When you consciously choose how to allocate your resources, you empower yourself to build a business that feels aligned, expansive, and sustainable.

Intentional Use of Resources and Achieving Goals

To create a thriving business, you must be intentional about how you allocate your resources, ensuring that you spend only what is necessary to achieve your desired results. Recognizing that you have a limited amount of time, energy, and money on any given day will help you make strategic decisions that align with your long-term vision.

As the leader of your business, it is your responsibility to make conscious decisions about where to invest or spend these precious resources. There are countless ways to allocate them, and the way you leverage each resource depends on the specific outcome you are trying to achieve.

To manage resources effectively, you must have clarity around:

- Your unique gifts and skills in business
- The overall vision for your business
- The specific goals you are working toward at this moment

Example: Growing Your Audience for a Launch

Imagine you are preparing for a launch of a new program aimed at helping mothers awaken their intuition. You want to grow your audience and generate leads within the next six weeks. You have two primary options:

1. **Using Time and Energy**
   - You choose to handle all aspects of audience growth and content creation yourself.
   - This requires working extra hours to manage both the content strategy and program development simultaneously.
   - Alternatively, you prioritize one task over the other, delaying the program launch due to time constraints.

2. **Using Money and Energy**
   - You invest in hiring a virtual assistant to help create and post content, which allows you to focus on developing the program.
   - This approach ensures your energy remains high, leading to better content quality and an increased ability to promote your program enthusiastically.
   - The likely outcome is a stronger audience response and a more successful launch.

Your resource management strategy should be a conscious choice based on your business goals, strengths, and available assets. By intentionally deciding how to allocate time, energy, and money, you create a business that not only thrives but also remains sustainable and aligned with your long-term vision.

Financial Planning

What Is Financial Planning?

Financial planning is the process of estimating future financial needs, setting budgets, forecasting revenues, and creating a strategy to ensure long-term business sustainability. It involves analyzing current finances, predicting future revenue and expenses, and making informed decisions about financial resource allocation.

The Importance of Financial Planning in Business

Financial planning is a crucial aspect of business success. Without a clear understanding of your finances, it is easy to overspend, underinvest, or make decisions that could negatively impact your business growth. Key benefits:

- **Sustainability:** Ensuring that your business remains financially healthy and operational over time
- **Profitability:** Making strategic decisions to maximize revenue and minimize unnecessary expenses
- **Investment Planning:** Understanding when and where to reinvest profits for growth
- **Risk Management:** Preparing for financial uncertainties and preventing cash flow crises

Key Aspects of Financial Planning for Entrepreneurs

Entrepreneurs must incorporate financial planning into their overall business strategy. Key components:

- **Budgeting**
  - Establishing a clear budget for expenses, operations, and growth initiatives
  - Differentiating between fixed costs (rent, salaries) and variable costs (marketing, software subscriptions)

- **Revenue Forecasting**
  - Predicting expected revenue streams based on past performance and market trends
  - Identifying high and low sales periods to plan financial reserves accordingly

- **Expense Management**
  - Tracking expenses to ensure financial efficiency
  - Identifying unnecessary spending and optimizing costs where possible

- **Cash Flow Planning**
  - Ensuring there is enough cash available to cover day-to-day business operations
  - Managing accounts receivable and payable efficiently

- **Funding and Investment Strategies**
  - Determining whether external funding (loans, investors) is needed
  - Reinvesting profits strategically to scale the business

Implementing Financial Planning

Entrepreneurs should incorporate financial planning into their business planning process regularly. This includes the following:

- Setting financial goals and tracking progress monthly or quarterly
- Using financial software or working with an accountant to maintain accurate records
- Adjusting forecasts based on market trends and business performance

Financial planning and forecasting are essential for making informed, strategic decisions that support long-term business growth. By proactively managing finances, entrepreneurs can ensure their business remains profitable, sustainable, and resilient against financial challenges.

CHAPTER 13

BRINGING YOUR BUSINESS VISION TO LIFE

The Process of Bringing Your Business Vision to Life

Building a sustainable, fulfilling, and profitable business is highly dependent on the level of clarity you have around what you are actually creating. Without clarity, execution becomes scattered, and progress feels slow or overwhelming. With clarity, you can move forward with intention and confidence, making strategic decisions that align with your long-term vision.

Now, you've done the work. You've gained clarity on your business, mapped out the core elements, and created an aligned business plan based on your Human Design. You understand your offers, your ideal clients, your marketing strategies, and the flow of your business operations. The pieces are in place. But now, the real challenge begins: implementation.

Owning Your Role as a Business Leader

As a business owner, leader, founder, and visionary, you are ultimately responsible for the success of your business. You get to define success. If you define success as having a fulfilling, profitable, and sustainable business, then creating a strategic business plan is the first step, regardless of what stage of business you are in.

Ultimately, if you want your future to be different from your present (without wasting time, energy, and money) you need a business plan. Full stop. A clear picture of what you are creating and how you will bring it to life eliminates the guesswork. You no longer wonder how to spend your time; you no longer leak energy that could be spent on joyful pursuits; and you no longer waste money on things that don't serve your ultimate goals.

Implementing Your Business Plan

The business plan you have developed is your roadmap. It is not meant to sit in a folder untouched; it is meant to guide your daily, weekly, and monthly actions. *Every* decision you make, from marketing to operations to client engagement, should align with the foundational plan you've created. The more you implement, the more tangible your vision becomes.

Your Client Journey: From Awareness to Loyalty

At its core, your business operates through a client journey, a sequence of activities that moves a person from not knowing you exist to becoming a loyal client who refers others to you. This journey includes the following:

1. **Attracting Attention:** Making potential clients aware of your brand through marketing, content, and outreach
2. **Building Connection:** Establishing trust through consistent messaging, engagement, and authenticity
3. **Converting Clients:** Helping people make the decision to work with you through an aligned sales process
4. **Delivering Value:** Providing an exceptional client experience through your offers and services
5. **Creating Loyalty:** Encouraging repeat clients and referrals by exceeding expectations and nurturing relationships

Managing Your Resources and Hiring Support

A thriving business requires effective resource management. This includes time, money, and energy. Knowing when to delegate tasks, hire support, and invest in systems is key to maintaining long-term sustainability.

- **Time Management:** Prioritize tasks that align with your highest-impact activities
- **Financial Management:** Allocate budgets strategically to support growth and scalability
- **Hiring Support:** Whether through contractors, team members, or automation tools, delegation allows you to stay focused on your strengths while ensuring efficiency.

The Gap Between Planning and Action

One of the biggest obstacles that entrepreneurs face is not the planning process itself but the act of bringing that plan to life. Some people don't follow through because they never created a plan in the first place, leaving them directionless and reactive rather than proactive. Others create a beautiful, detailed plan and then hesitate to execute it.

Why does this happen? The answer often lies in the intersection of uncertainty and self-doubt. When something is new, whether it's a new business, a new offer, or a new approach, it naturally triggers doubt. The mind questions: *Can I really do this? Will this work? What if I fail?* These doubts create a mental block that keeps many entrepreneurs from taking the next step.

Overcoming the Doubt Barrier

Doubt is not a sign that you are on the wrong path. It is a natural response to stepping into something bigger than what you've done before. However, allowing doubt to dictate your actions can leave your vision stuck on paper instead of becoming a thriving reality.

This is where having a strong support system becomes critical. The truth is, belief is often borrowed before it is owned. Before you fully trust in your ability to bring your vision to life, you need people around you who already believe in you. These are the people who remind you of your strengths, reflect back to you the impact you're here to make, and hold the vision with you even when self-doubt creeps in.

Shifting from Hesitation to Action

Once you recognize the role that doubt plays, you can begin shifting your mindset and behaviors to take intentional action. Here's how:

1. **Reconnect with Your Why:** Revisit the deeper purpose behind your business. What impact do you want to create? How does this business serve your long-term vision?
2. **Break It Down:** Big visions can feel overwhelming. Break your plan into smaller, tangible steps; focus on one action at a time.
3. **Embrace Imperfect Action:** Waiting until you feel 100 percent ready will keep you stuck. Confidence is built through action, not before it.
4. **Seek Support:** Reach out to your network for encouragement, guidance, and perspective.
5. **Trust Your Design:** You have created a plan aligned with your unique energy. Trust that following your design will lead to the most easeful and expansive path forward.

The Power of Having a Clear Plan

Consider the following scenarios:

- **The Coaching Certification Temptation:** You see an amazing coaching certification marketed by the top influencer in your field. It looks incredible, and you wonder if you should invest. But when you refer to your business plan, you realize that it doesn't fit your priorities right now. You confidently say no, knowing you're staying aligned with your vision.
- **The Course Creation Struggle:** You are working on creating a course as a primary income stream in your business. It's been a year, and you're struggling to complete it. You've debated

whether to hire a coach to guide you or bring on a contractor to handle the parts that don't light you up. After having gone through the Aligned Business Blueprint process, you know exactly what choice aligns best with your goals, your Human Design, and your plan.

- **Investing with Confidence:** Decision-making becomes easy when you have clarity. You no longer second-guess yourself because you have a clear framework that guides your actions. Whether it's hiring support, launching a new offer, or pivoting your strategy, you now have the tools to make empowered choices that align with your ultimate business vision.

The Power of a Support System

Entrepreneurship is not meant to be a solo journey. Successful entrepreneurs surround themselves with a network of support, whether it's a mentor, a coach, a team, or a community of like-minded individuals. Here are some key support roles to consider:

- **Coaches and Mentors:** A coach helps you navigate your doubts, refine your strategies, and hold you accountable. A mentor provides wisdom from experience, showing you the road ahead.
- **Team Members and Contractors:** Trying to do everything alone is a fast track to burnout. Hiring the right people—whether employees, virtual assistants, or specialized contractors—allows you to stay in your zone of genius.
- **Business Besties and Community:** Surrounding yourself with fellow entrepreneurs who understand the ups and downs of business ownership can be incredibly grounding and motivating.
- **Trusted Friends and Family:** Even if they don't fully understand the intricacies of your business, their emotional support and encouragement can be invaluable.

Taking Action: Mapping Out Your Calendar

Now that you've created a well-thought-out business plan, you have all the pieces of the puzzle in place. You know what you're offering, who you're serving, and how you'll reach them. But a plan alone won't bring your vision to life; it's the implementation that transforms it from an idea into reality.

The next step is to intentionally map out your calendar. This isn't just about time management; it's about creating a client journey that feels aligned for both you and your prospective clients. A business that operates in flow doesn't happen by accident, it's built through conscious choices about when and how you take action.

What Your Written Business Plan Has Given You

At this stage, your business plan has provided two critical layers of clarity:

1. **Clarity on the actions:** You now have a clear vision of what needs to be done to move your business forward.
2. **Clarity on who is responsible for the actions:** Whether it's you or your team, you've outlined who is executing each piece of the plan.

But there's one more layer that's essential for success: Clarity on *when* you're doing the actions.

Without an intentional schedule, even the best business plan can fall flat. To bring your vision to life, you need to integrate key dates and time blocks into your calendar. This ensures that your business runs smoothly, your launches happen with ease, and you're not constantly operating in reactive mode.

Here are some key elements to schedule:

- **Start dates of programs:** When are your offers available to clients? Whether you run live programs, evergreen courses, or a mix, knowing these dates helps you plan marketing and delivery.

- **Launch periods:** When will you be actively promoting? Planning your launch windows ahead of time ensures you have enough time to create content, engage your audience, and drive sales.
- **Dedicated time for each area of business:** Every aspect of your business needs intentional focus. Block out time for:
  - Offer and program development
  - Marketing (content creation, visibility, and outreach)
  - Sales activities (calls, email sequences, and promotions)
  - Service delivery (client work, group calls, and support)

Your Plan Is the Foundation, Implementation Is the Creation

Think of your business plan as the blueprint for your success. But just like a house, having the blueprint isn't enough, you have to actually build it. Your calendar is the structure that turns the vision into something tangible.

This step isn't about rigid scheduling or forcing yourself into an unnatural rhythm. It's about designing a workflow that aligns with your Human Design, your energy cycles, and the way you love to work. When your calendar reflects your values and your strengths, your business will feel more expansive, intentional, and sustainable.

By mapping out your calendar with clarity and purpose, you're setting yourself up for a business that flows with ease, one where you can show up fully, serve your clients powerfully, and grow in a way that feels aligned.

Your Business, Your Legacy

Bringing your business vision to life is not just about executing a plan—it's about stepping into the fullest expression of your purpose. It's about showing up, taking aligned action, and allowing your impact to unfold. Every successful entrepreneur started where you are now: with an idea, a plan, and the choice to move forward despite uncertainty.

Your business has the potential to transform lives, including your own. Trust that the vision was given to you for a reason. With a solid plan, the right support, and a commitment to taking action, you will bring your business vision to life in ways that exceed even your greatest expectations.

Now, it's time to bring your business vision to life.

Living and Embodying a New Reality

There is an emotional waterfall that happens when you commit to alignment. And sharing emotion has been part of the great lesson I have been learning throughout my life and also as a business leader. Several times throughout my personal and professional evolutions, I experienced overwhelming feelings of fear, excitement, overwhelm, and gratitude. Each time I make a conscious decision to lean deeper into alignment, the uncomfortable things I haven't wanted to face were stirred up and staring me in the face. These were the areas I needed to heal through, grow through, and expand through to make that next level a reality.

The emotional side of entrepreneurship is wild y'all. There is a season when you don't believe in yourself or what you are creating. There is a season when you start to believe more in yourself, but maybe you are still not fully clear on what you are building. Then, a season comes when the vision you had is actually starting to become reality, and the emotional roller coaster continues. Whatever season you may be in, I encourage you to remember that seasons are always changing. It's important to find a balance of enjoying where you are, with also being intentional about what is coming next. Because, as you grow, your business grows. As your business grows, you are propelled to grow as an entrepreneur as well. Some of these seasons will feel like sipping sparkling water by the pool, while others will feel like you are walking through a hailstorm. This is my reminder to you that you get to choose how you show up always and how you choose to interpret each season. In much of the success I have experienced in my life, I can see threads of lessons from the hailstorms and celebrations from the pool that were equally important in helping me become the person that could confidently lead at that level of success.

The most important message I can leave you with is this: *Business is personal.* I have seen this over and over, whether it was being a leader in the corporate world or in the entrepreneurial world. We are souls here with unique missions and callings, so every decision and action we take in this lifetime is a reflection of our abilities and awareness at that time. That is deeply personal to each of us and our unique missions. So, understanding that emotions may be potentially impacting your decisions and actions is critical for your entrepreneurial journey (this is for everyone, not just the people with Emotional Authorities). Our conditioning and beliefs around success, progress, and achievement are fundamentally important to explore as entrepreneurs. And this is why I believe that strategic, intentional, and aligned planning is critical to helping you stay focused and be intentional with how you move forward in your business.

Learning how to connect with my own emotions has been a huge part of my expansion this season. I began to accept my frustration, and finally listened to my Not-Self telling me it was time to leave my small, rural hometown and move to the city. I allowed myself to face the fear that came with following a path different from the one my parents wanted for me, that my employers pointed me toward, or even the one I thought I once wanted. I even let go of all of the coaching programs that I invested in and here I am following a path and plan that doesn't look like any of theirs.

I can share countless stories of entrepreneurs feeling stuck, stagnant, and lost, wondering what their next step was in business. This is your reminder that business is not a guessing game; it is an alignment game. Human Design has been the validation I have been seeking from the outside, when I was not yet ready to trust myself and my own path. I am here to show you that you can indeed trust yourself and create an aligned business unique to you.

Since the moment I wrote the first version of my business plan for the Spiritual Business Incubator LLC, my business has seen the fastest growth and most progress in the shortest amount of time. And the beginning was way more emotionally turbulent than I ever expected. Still, I sit here writing the conclusion to this book, which once was an idea that landed inside of a business plan. There is something powerful about taking a bunch of ideas, intentionally aligning them with your mission, and then seeing those ideas come to life. This is what I have experienced at exponential speed since writing the first business plan for the Spiritual Business Incubator. I am so focused on where I am putting my time and energy, building a structure and team that suports my unique design, and also enjoying the journey along the way.

Gaining full clarity—on exactly who I am, what I am creating at a soul-level, and how I am going to create it in alignment—has been the key to my ability to make sustainable progress while also staying confident in the future of my business. My ultimate wish for anyone reading this book is this: confidence in the future of your aligned business. I wrote this book and poured my wisdom, passion, and soul into these pages so you can create your uniquely purposeful and profitable path as well.

This combination is where real-life magic happens.

Through my experience, I am certain that all of the strategies work; you just have to find the ones that are aligned to you and your mission. Because when you consciously take the time to slow down and complete the business planning process with intention, you are doing more than writing a document. You are energetically grounding your vision in reality. The statistics already show that old school business planning is extremely effective, and now in the new age, we get to weave in things like Human Design, Gene Keys, astrology, numerology, and more. With all of this combined, I believe that the impact of businesses in the future will be exponentially amplified. By creating an aligned business, you are taking an idea that was once a channeled message, a quantum idea particle, or a seed of inspiration, and you are planting it in this 3D reality. Bridging divine inspiration with strategic business planning is a magical, practical, intentional way of making the world a better place.

For me, getting into alignment meant moving myself, my husband, and kiddos to a new city 200 miles away from where we grew up. It meant walking away from prestigious opportunities that looked good on paper but drained my soul. It meant owning my gifts and healing the wounds that kept me from sharing them. It meant growing as a person and as a leader, even if that meant doing things that felt scary. It meant being brave enough to bring forward my thought leadership and set higher standards for the future of entrepreneurship. Most importantly, it meant committing to myself and the vision on my heart, for my life and for my business.

Thank you for trusting me to lead you on this journey, and until next time my friend, cheers to your success!

ADDITIONAL RESOURCES

If you're feeling inspired to dive deeper into Human Design and the energetics of aligned business, I've gathered a curated list of my favorite foundational Human Design books and other powerful resources that have shaped my journey. Whether you're just beginning or ready to explore more advanced teachings, you'll find trusted titles to support your growth and integration.

Visit spiritualbusinessincubator.com/books to explore the full list and start building your own aligned resource library.

ABOUT THE AUTHOR

Anna Nichols is the founder of the Spiritual Business Incubator™, where she helps mission-driven entrepreneurs bring their visionary legacies to life by blending practical business strategy with an innovative infusion of Human Design. With a Master's Degree in Business, 15+ years of business development experience, and her unique expertise as a leader in the Human Design for Business industry, Anna guides entrepreneurs to feel confident in exactly who they are, gain clarity on the kind of business they are meant to build, and take step-by-step action to make it a reality.

Her entrepreneurial roots run deep, beginning at age ten while working in her Polish immigrant parents' hotel, and have evolved into a career dedicated to helping others design purposeful, profitable, and soul-aligned businesses. Today, she is a thought leader, the host of the *Design and Align Your Business* podcast, and is releasing her first book with Human Design Press.

As a 5/2 Sacral Generator with the Left Angle Cross of Cycles & Development, Anna is designed to initiate powerful new beginnings, create momentum, and help others break through limitations. Her mission is to support heart-led visionaries in stepping into their most magnetic role, building sustainable businesses, and raising the vibration of the collective.

SpiritualBusinessIncubator.com

For more great books from Human Design Press

Visit Books.GracePointPublishing.com

HUMAN
DESIGN
PRESS

If you enjoyed reading *Create Your Aligned Business,* and purchased it through an online re-
tailer, please return to the site and write a review to help others find the book.

www.ingramcontent.com/pod-product-compliance
Lightning Source LLC
Chambersburg PA
CBHW071556210326
41597CB00019B/3264